Designing the
Communication Experiment

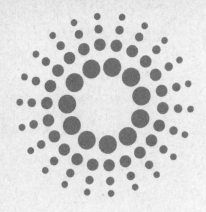

*Studies in
Speech*

CONTRIBUTING
EDITOR

Don Geiger
UNIVERSITY OF
CALIFORNIA,
BERKELEY

Designing the Communication Experiment

John Waite Bowers

University of Iowa

Random House

NEW YORK

Foreword

The remarkable growth of the social sciences has not been accompanied by a corresponding growth in concern for the understanding of the layman and the neophyte. Learning the processes, as opposed to the outcomes, of social research has been left for the graduate level. Some students, of course, do learn earlier what science is and when a generalization can be recognized as "scientific." They do so, however, only if they are gifted enough to infer a formal process from concrete instances or if they are fortunate enough to encounter a teacher who can explain the process clearly.

The absence of books to acquaint undergraduates with the scientific process and the scientific attitude is especially surprising in view of social science's ubiquitous concern with communication. The lure of the laboratory for the social scientist is very strong, of course; yet it should not be so strong that it prevents him from taking steps to insure that future social scientists will be well equipped with fundamentals. The most fundamental of the fundamentals is understanding the scientific process.

This book treats science in an introductory way. It treats especially scientific problems in communication, though the early chapters are more general and, for that matter, the later chapters can be used as specimens of the process with relevance for any of the social sciences. Because the book is an introduction, it eschews the argots of particular social sciences, including the statistical argot, except when those special vocabularies are essential and easily explainable. It tells the uninitiated and the confused what social science is all about.

John Waite Bowers

MAY 1969

v

Contents

Designing the
Communication Experiment

1

The
Scientific
Method

If any statement in contemporary American civilization demands respect, it is one beginning with the sanction, "Scientific research has shown that . . ." The word "science" connotes to us machinelike men patiently pursuing intellectual quests for more destructive weapons and more effective toothpastes, and menlike machines furiously clicking and shimmering in their never-ending tasks of assimilating, processing, and analyzing data to produce infallible generalizations. The scientist in his laboratory wears a white coat, and his verbalizations borrow its purity. He and his work are cloaked in mystery, but he has been right so often and his discoveries have been so useful that to doubt his veracity would be ingratitude. He is the man who wins wars, puts men on the moon, investigates riots, prevents floods, predicts elections. Because we usually cannot do these things ourselves, we tend to attribute such accomplishments to a strange apparatus and a unique way of thinking.

The aim of this chapter is to describe science in a way that dispels the aura of mystery surrounding it.[1] Science is not merely apparatus and white coats. It is a method of explaining and ultimately predicting events. Science is not a strange or unique method. It is the same method almost all of us use most of the time in our day-to-day intellectual existence. The only difference is that the scientific method is systematic and social. It takes the best characteristics of individual thought and makes the resulting system a cultural artifact.

Like individual thought, science requires a set of rules for its operation. It demands some kinds of activities, permits others, and forbids still others. The following hypothetical account of an event and its consequences for three individuals will introduce these rules.

THREE WAYS OF EXPLAINING EVENTS

After the Fall but before history, three men clothed in skins are sitting in a circle. (For convenience, we will call the three men Martin, Calvin, and Isaac.) Thundershowers that occurred the night before have produced a chill in the air, and Martin suggests they utilize some recently acquired technology to build a fire. Calvin and Isaac agree. They build the fire and warmth returns to the circle.

Resting partly in the fire is a saucer-shaped rock that the thundershowers have filled with water. After a few minutes of conversation, Isaac notices that the water in the rock has begun to bubble. He watches the water carefully until its bubbling becomes violent. He calls the phenomenon to the attention of Martin and Calvin.

Martin creeps toward the fire, inspects his surroundings, looks questioningly at Calvin and Isaac, and gingerly touches the water with his index finger. He withdraws immediately, shrieks with pain, and retreats wildly to the mouth of his cave. His companions observe his activities but, noticing no ill effects to themselves, remain in their places and induce Martin to return. A discussion of the event ensues.

MARTIN   Stay away from that water. The fire god had a baby. The baby is in that water. The baby god bit my finger almost like the fire god does when you get too close to it. He might bite you too.

CALVIN   Martin, you always take things too personally. We know the fire god is a man, and we know men don't have babies.

MARTIN   The fire god had a baby. I felt the bite.

CALVIN   Babies don't bite. They don't have any teeth.

MARTIN   (nonplussed by this logic)   If fire god's baby didn't bite me, why does my finger hurt?

CALVIN   Martin, you must learn to see things from a broader perspective. Now think. The purpose of water is to disappear. Water is always going someplace. Even when it stands perfectly still it disappears. The water in this rock has been here too long. It must disappear. That's what it's *for*. That bubbling just helps it disappear faster. Look, you can see much of it gone already. It didn't hurt you because of any baby god that dislikes you. It hurt you because you interfered with its purpose. It would hurt anybody who did that. Things always hurt people when people get in the way of their goals. I agree that we should stay away from that water. But not because of any baby god.

MARTIN   I still think the fire god had a baby and put it in that water. Or maybe the fire god is in that water himself.

CALVIN   What makes you think so?

MARTIN   It bit me.

Martin and Calvin, left to themselves, might continue their conversation throughout the day and far into the night. They have said enough, however, to permit us to label their apparently characteristic ways of explaining events—the frames of reference for their respective perceptions.

Martin's approach may be called *animistic*. Martin attributes the event of the boiling water to a being that he asserts to be present but unobservable or, possibly, observable only to himself. Although this position may give Martin a sense of satisfaction in his own importance, it probably will not facilitate his development as a scientist. Calvin and Isaac have no way of checking Martin's explanation, because gods normally are not amenable to observation. If Calvin and Isaac accept the animistic interpretation, they might touch the water with their fingers to discover whether the god bites them too. When they find that he does, they will cease their inquiry.

Calvin's interpretation is *teleological*. He asserts that everything has its purpose and that events can be explained in terms of that purpose. Calvin responds to Martin's pain by saying, essentially, "It's all for the best." Although Calvin's explanation might give him (and us) more verbal satisfaction than Martin's does, it will discourage science just as effectively. If we accept the teleological frame of reference, we will discontinue inquiry as soon as we can think of a purpose that is compatible with an event. Occasionally, this kind of reasoning might trick us into attributing contradictory purposes to the same things. (For example, Martin might ask, "If the purpose of water is to disappear, why does rain fall?") But we almost always can talk our way out of such contradictions. ("If water's purpose is to disappear, it has to appear first, doesn't it?")

We can detect certain similarities between animistic and teleological explanations. The most salient one is that both explanations are primarily subjective rather than primarily objective. We invent them; we do not discover them. They do not include in their rules a requirement that their generalizations be put to the test of observation. Animism permits great subjective latitude. It puts no limit on the number and kind of beings we might devise to answer the recurrent question, "Why did that happen?" Teleology is slightly more limited to facts because it requires purpose and because our notion of purpose comes from observation of ourselves. Thus a teleological explanation, based on our experience with purposive beings, is less likely than an animistic one to violate our observations in an extreme way.

To say that animistic and teleological explanations are subjective and scientifically sterile is not to say that they are wrong either generally or in any given case. They may be right. Certainly, they are occasionally satisfying. But they are not testable, and the scientist insists on the possibility of testing explanations.

Obviously, the hero of our story is Isaac. During his friends' discussion, he has been observing closely the fire, the rock, and the water. When the debate reaches an impasse, he picks up a branch and asks Martin and Calvin to help him move the now less-than-full rock away from the fire. They comply, and the water stops bubbling. ("The baby god wants to stay close to its parent," says Martin.) Isaac asks Martin and Calvin to help him move the rock back to the fire. They do. Shortly, the water resumes its bubbling.

Under Isaac's direction, the trio find another dish-shaped rock, fill it with water, and place it near the fire. In a few minutes, they notice the same violence in the water. "I think," says Isaac, "that when water in a rock is placed near this fire, it bubbles and disappears even more rapidly than usual. I wonder if it will do the same thing near another fire."

By this time Martin and Calvin, having participated in Isaac's research, are interested. They cooperate to build another fire some distance from the first. Repeating their procedures from the first study, they note the same phenomenon in the water. They have now used four rocks and two fires, always with the same results.

"That takes care of your argument against me, Calvin," says Martin. "The fire god is a man, but the rock god is a woman. The rock god had the baby. The fire god is the father. The baby is a boy, so it wants to stay close to its father. That's why it leaves the water when we move its mother away from its father."

Isaac has not yet completed his research. "Unless I'm mistaken," he says, "water will bubble when we place it near a fire regardless of the vessel that contains it." He, Martin, and Calvin search for and find some other natural vessels suitable for holding water—a bone, a piece of petrified wood. The new vessels do not affect the results.

"An interesting discovery," says Martin. "Gods of all hollow vessels are female."

"It proves my point," says Calvin. "Water, when placed near

fire, wants to disappear more quickly. Bubbling helps it do that."

"Water, when placed near fire, bubbles violently and disappears quickly," says Isaac. "Also, when touched, it may cause pain, but I'm not sure of that yet."

Isaac has taken a *deterministic* position. He asserts that observable events are related functionally, in ways that make their discovery and prediction possible. He disregards Martin's talk of gods and Calvin's talk of purposes. Any generalizations he makes will be derived from observations, although, of course, these generalizations will go beyond the observations. (Isaac cannot hope to observe all the water in the world in all the hollow vessels in the world near all the fires in the world.) The reason he makes generalizations is to enable him to predict future events. This ability to predict may at times be useful to him, but as a determinist he does not perceive the possible utility of this ability as its chief value. He considers the ability to predict desirable for its own sake. This way of explaining events is the foundation of science, and Isaac's methods make him as much a scientist as Galileo or Newton.

THE SCIENTIFIC PROCESS

Science is a systematic search for functional relationships between antecedents and their consequents. Its purpose is prediction, and everything in the method contributes to achieving that purpose. The following discussion will contain mention of the following terms, which, if assimilated, will contribute greatly to understanding the scientific process and, as an application of that process, the communication experiment: *fact, hypothesis, field study, experiment, independent variable, dependent variable, replicability* and *operationism, control, law, theory, validity,* and *elegance.*

Martin, Calvin, and Isaac were all privy to the same *facts*— that is, they made observations about which, as competent observers, they agreed. They all saw a vessel containing water close to a fire. They all saw the water bubble violently. Such facts, agreed-upon observations, are the beginnings of science.

All three men made guesses about the meaning or significance of the facts they observed. Martin invented a mythology, Calvin invented a teleology. But Isaac's guess can be dignified with the name *hypothesis:* A hypothesis is a guess about the functional relationship between antecedents and consequents that is testable by observation. Isaac's first hypothesis was that the nearness of the water to the fire and the boiling of the water were functionally related. To test this hypothesis, he made a prediction from it: If the water is moved away from the fire, it will cease bubbling. Isaac ultimately confirmed his hypothesis. If the water had continued to boil at a considerable distance from the fire, his observations would have forced him to discard that guess and try another. Probably, he would have tried to move the water from that rock to another, operating according to the hypothesis that the rock and the boiling were functionally related.

Isaac's first observations, before he and his friends moved the water away from the fire, constituted part of what might be called a *field study*. Field studies are attempts to derive functional relationships from systematic observations of events as they occur uncontrolled in nature. Field studies are one way of furthering science, though usually not the most efficient way. Like other methods of establishing functional relationships, they require hypotheses and hypothesis-testing. For example, Isaac might have observed the initial boiling of the water and guessed that the nearness to the fire and the boiling were a functionally related antecedent and its consequent. He might then have decided to test his hypothesis by continuing his observation until the fire had died down completely. If he were correct in his guess, the water should have stopped boiling. This observation of an uncontrolled natural event would confirm his hypothesis. However, the confirmation would not be definite, for the almost simultaneous disappearance of the fire and the bubbling might be just a coincidence. In other words, the functional antecedent of the boiling might be something other than the fire, something Isaac failed to observe. Maybe the fire went out just at dark, and the functional relationship of the boiling was with light and darkness. Maybe a tree fell at the moment the water stopped boiling, and the functional relationship was with the health of the tree. Maybe Martin and Calvin left just before the water stopped boiling, and the functional relationship was with their presence.

Instead of depending on such uncertainties, Isaac used an alternative, preferred method of hypothesis-testing. He devised a series of *experiments* in an attempt to confirm his hypothesis that the antecedent (nearness to the fire) was functionally related to the consequent (boiling) by *controlling* all the other antecedents he could think of. His reasoning went this way: If the water boils when it is near the fire but does not boil when it is away from the fire, then nearness to the fire and boiling are functionally related. When Isaac moved the rock away from the fire (the control condition), then back, and observed the expected activity in the water, he satisfied himself that this reasoning was correct. The antecedent and consequent varied concomitantly.[2]

In experimental work like Isaac's, and sometimes in field studies, the suspected antecedent (nearness to the fire) is called the *independent variable*. The consequent (boiling) will not occur without the independent variable, so the suspected consequent is referred to as the *dependent variable*.

Isaac is not yet satisfied, for he sees that his generalization is only a weak one. Possibly, the functional relationship he has confirmed through his experiment is specific to that particular rock, that particular fire, and that particular water. To increase generalizability, he conducts a series of experiments, changing in each case his independent variable. First he tries a different rock. Boiling occurs. Therefore, type of rock appears not to enter into the relationship between antecedent and consequent. Then he tries a different fire and different water. Boiling occurs. Therefore, type of fire and source of water appear not to enter into the relationship between antecedent and consequent. Finally, he manipulates vessels other than rocks as his independent variable. Boiling occurs. Therefore, type of vessel does not influence the relationship between antecedent and consequent. Because none of these variables must be used to qualify his statement, he feels secure in making the relatively powerful generalization: "Water, when placed near fire, bubbles violently and disappears quickly." This kind of statement, one that relates at least one set of antecedent facts to at least one set of consequent facts, may be called a *law*.

Isaac's experiments meet the scientific requirement of *replicability*. Isaac has enabled others, given similar materials, to repeat his procedures and observations by *operationism*. He can specify the procedures another must follow to manipulate the same variables in the same way with, presumably, the same result. Isaac can say: "If you go to such-and-such a place and dip out some of the liquid there, you will have what I mean by 'water.' If you strike this rock on that mineral over this kind of wood shavings, and if thereafter you observe the wood shavings burst into flame, you will have what I mean by 'fire.' If you find a natural object shaped concavely, and if you turn the object so that the concavity is at the top, you will have what I mean by 'vessel.' If you place the vessel filled with water within a finger's breadth of the flames, you will have it in a position I call 'near the fire.' " The cruciality of operationism and replicability to science will become apparent later in this section.

The hypothetical story is continued to illustrate the scientific process. Millenniums pass. Gordon, Bernard, Charlotte, and Joan are American Indians indigent to parts of what is now the United States not yet occupied by whites. Gordon lives in what is now Iowa City, Iowa; Bernard and Charlotte, a brother and sister, live in what is now Denver, Colorado; Joan lives near what is now Death Valley, California.

The four meet during a continental convention held in what is now Lawrence, Kansas to decide on policies to follow toward the whites who have recently settled on the East Coast. After the council, they happen to find themselves seated around the same campfire and soon discover that they share a deterministic attitude. Most of the talk relates incidents in which they have debunked witch doctors in their respective tribes.

Eventually, they begin discussing their other accomplishments. Gordon (anticipating Fahrenheit) mentions that he has recently discovered a way to measure heat with mercury in a hollow tube and that he has been able to manufacture and calibrate identically two such instruments. He relates a few of the experiments he has carried out with it, noting that he has established as a scientific law the statement: "Water, when heated to 212 degrees, boils."

(We recognize, of course, that Gordon's law is not new. It is only a refinement of Isaac's law. The invention of a new instrument for measurement has simply enabled Gordon to make that law more precise. Inventions often enable greater precision in scientific laws, and like the telescope, they occasionally make possible the testing of previously untestable hypotheses and the formulation of new laws.)

During the discussion, Charlotte has changed her position in the circle so that she is now seated next to Gordon. She expresses great admiration for Gordon's accomplishments with his new instrument and indicates that she would like to see it work. Her brother Bernard, however, expresses strong skepticism and implies that Gordon's talk is intended primarily to impress Charlotte. Joan holds her peace for the most part, though Charlotte notices that she nods occasionally when Bernard goes on the attack.

As is the way with scientists, Gordon invites Bernard to dispel his own skepticism by the only method available under the rules of science, observation. Bernard accepts the invitation, and Gordon agrees to send his spare thermometer to Denver via the next messenger from Iowa City. He puts in writing his operational definitions, gives them to Bernard, and gets Charlotte to assure him that she will check, and if necessary replicate, Bernard's manipulations and observations. The four drink a final toast to the supremacy of fact and disperse to their homes in Iowa, Colorado, and California.

Months pass, during which Bernard occasionally expresses his belief that no such instrument as a thermometer exists. But finally the messenger from Iowa City arrives with a cylindrical parcel for Bernard and Charlotte.

With no delay, Bernard finds the notes on procedure that

Gordon gave him at the conference. With Charlotte's help, he builds his fire and begins to conduct his research. The mercury hovers around 203 degrees when the water begins to boil but does not rise beyond that. At Charlotte's insistence, they repeat the experiment with the same result.

Tom-toms sound the message across Kansas, Nebraska, and Iowa: "Gordon: Your law wrong. Congrats to me for correcting. Water boils when heated to 203 degrees. Bernard's law."

Needless to say, Gordon does not accept Bernard's correction kindly. His own research, which has been proceeding smoothly, depends on the law that water boils when it is heated to 212 degrees. As a scientist, however, Gordon knows that his only recourse is to observation. If Bernard has observed repeatedly that water boils at 203 degrees and if Charlotte has checked his observations as she had agreed to do, then he must search for hypotheses to explain the difference between his results and Bernard's. He knows that speculation must always give way to fact.

First, he asks one of his colleagues in Iowa City to replicate his own experiments. The colleague does and finds that water repeatedly boils at a temperature very near 212 degrees. Still, Gordon is not satisfied that a real difference exists between Bernard's law and his law. He thinks that the fault may be in the measuring instrument.

The next messenger from Iowa City to Denver carries Gordon's thermometer and a message instructing Bernard to send the other thermometer back. Bernard also reads about the procedures Gordon has followed in replicating his experiments and the results derived from them.

Within a year, the exchange of thermometers is effected. The experiments are repeated. The tom-toms sound, and both Gordon and Bernard know that the relationship between their respective laws remains one of conflict. The intensity of the emotional tone in the messages begins to increase in a negative direction.

Charlotte, of course, holds both men in high esteem. She is concerned with what seems to be a deteriorating relationship that can have nothing but bad effects for her. Also, as a scientist, she knows that invective will never solve the empirical question: At what temperature does water boil?

On the one hand, she has witnessed Bernard's experiments and has seen water boil repeatedly at 203 degrees. On the other hand, Gordon's reports of his studies are perfectly credible to her. She knows him to be a conscientious scientist, and, even if he were not, she knows that he would not dare to falsify a law when others could so easily detect the deceit through observation. She is strongly motivated to seek an explanation compatible with both laws.

Charlotte confines herself for a month, during which she ponders the differences between Gordon's studies and Bernard's. She discards, on the basis of her own informal observations, the idea that fires are hotter in Iowa City than in Denver. She discards, a little reluctantly, the untestable idea that the nature of Denver water is to be always cooler than Iowa City water, other conditions being equal.

On the thirtieth day of her confinement, Charlotte manages to express an idea that has been gestating in her mind. Once again, the tom-toms sound between Denver and Iowa City: "Gordon: Could it be that the temperature at which water boils decreases with westerly movement? As always, Charlotte."

Gordon immediately accepts the generalization and publishes it among his friends as "Charlotte's Theory." A *theory* is a statement or a set of statements that relates functionally at least two sets of laws. It differs from a law only in its scope and its generality. Like a law, a theory must contain the seeds of its own destruction—that is, it must generate predictions testable by observation. The experiments to which these predictions give rise must have in them the potential for producing results that could lead to the modification or discarding of the theory.

Charlotte's theory meets these criteria reasonably well. It is much more general than either of the two previously incompatible laws it attempts to relate. Furthermore, it directly generates a great number of hypotheses that, if discarded, will lead to its own alteration or destruction.

Bernard is less sanguine about the theory than Gordon proved to be. Knowing his sister, he perceives the possibility that her attempt to conciliate the two laws might be more instrumental for her in a personal way than in a scientific way. The two discuss possibilities for providing an efficient test of the theory.

Bernard remembers that Joan participated in the original discussion and expresses the opinion that she could be enlisted to cooperate. Inferring from Charlotte's theory, he observes that Denver is about as far west of Iowa City as Death Valley is west of Denver. If Charlotte's theory works, the temperature at which water boils in Death Valley should be about as far below the temperature at which water boils in Denver as that temperature is below the temperature at which water boils in Iowa City. This calculation puts the hypothetical boiling temperature for water in Death Valley at 194 degrees.

Bernard immediately dispatches a messenger for Joan, sending the thermometer, operational definitions and procedural instructions, the history of the controversy, and a closing statement expressing the hope that he and she might meet to discuss the results. Joan receives the message, notes the possible implications to be inferred from the closing statement, and does her experiments.

In a few days, the tom-toms carry a message from Death Valley to Denver, thence to Iowa City: "Bernard and all: Charlotte's theory worse than bad. Water here boils at almost 213 degrees in repeated experiments. I have found answer. Meet me at peace convention next year for details. Fondly, Joan."

Charlotte's theory failed to meet the test of *validity*. In other words, the theory failed to produce accurate predictions. In fact, it failed so badly that rather than attempt to modify it to fit the new data, Joan decided to discard it totally and to start from scratch with the still incompatible laws.

Bernard sees in Joan's message the beginning of a friendly rivalry. As soon as the thermometer is returned, he goes to work. He begins to travel as widely as he can, repeating the experiment at the conclusion of each day's trek, and he sends

Gordon a message asking him to do the same. Both men keep careful records of their locations and boiling points. Between them, they travel the breadth of the continent, taking measurements at daily intervals. They arrange to arrive at the peace convention a day early to discuss their findings.

Still responding to Charlotte's theory when they meet, they devise a chart showing boiling temperatures as a function of position on the continent (see Figure 1).

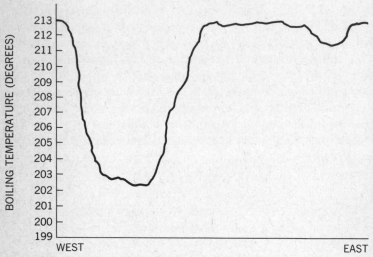

Figure 1 Boiling Temperature as a Function of Geographical Location

When the four meet around their campfire, Bernard and Gordon proudly produce their chart. Bernard makes the presentation:

> When Gordon and I heard Joan's report, we perceived immediately that Charlotte's theory needed adjustment. For that reason, we thought that gathering of more data would be desirable. Because boiling temperature is obviously in some way a function of geographical location, we decided to travel across the continent, performing the boiling experiment at regular

intervals. Charting our data geographically, we saw that they fit an irregular curve that we hereby publish. We think that this curve amounts to a theory from which we can predict the boiling temperature of water at any point on a path across the central part of the continent, moving from east to west.

The two ladies applaud, and Gordon and Bernard receive their congratulations with becoming modesty.

Then Joan asks for attention:

To my colleagues, I can do nothing but express my admiration for their ingenuity and my envy for their industry. Their scientific contribution will certainly prove to be significant.

However, I would like to propose an alternative to their theory. When I received the instructions and the account of the conflicting laws, together with Charlotte's theory, I fully expected my little experiment simply to substantiate the theory of another. My surprise was great when the experiment not only failed to substantiate the theory but even partially contradicted it. I therefore searched for explanations other than geographical location.

You all know that I lay no claim to genius. Only the most obvious possibilities occurred to me. In effect, I asked the question: Will variations in environment that may change my physical feelings also change the temperature at which the water boils? I therefore tried the experiment in the sun, in the shade, in the wigwam, even on a raft in the water. These manipulations did not significantly affect the boiling temperature.

As you know, Death Valley is located near a very high mountain. The mountain is always in my vision. When climbing the mountain, I have noticed difficulty in breathing, even more difficulty than the physical exertion by itself would explain. As I gazed at the mountain, I wondered whether water would boil at the same temperature on top of it as in my valley.

I therefore decided to investigate. Taking a friend with me, I climbed the mountain. Whenever we could find a convenient place, we repeated the experiment, I observing and she checking my observations. My hypothesis was that boiling temperature and the distance we climbed would be functionally related.

Imagine my delight when I discovered that as we climbed higher, our experiments yielded regularly different results. Soon we began to predict specific boiling temperatures at the various heights we reached. Our predictions were most accurate.

As a result of this research, I feel justified in expressing the following generalization, which, I think, is superior as a theory in some ways even to that of Bernard and Gordon:

The temperature at which water boils is an inverse function of altitude. It decreases at the rate of about one degree every 500 feet.

My colleagues should not take this theory or this speech as a belittlement of their accomplishments. Their data can be most valuable in checking the validity of my theory. All we need to do is recalculate a little, predicting their results from my theory by using altitude rather than east-west axis as the independent variable. No better test for the theory could be devised. Again, I congratulate them.

Joan takes her seat next to Bernard to the accompaniment of sustained applause. An inspection of their data does indeed confirm the theory.

Joan's theory, unlike Charlotte's, proves to be valid. It generates accurate predictions. Bernard and Gordon's theory is also valid, though possibly not quite as accurate as Joan's. Yet Joan's theory seems to be far superior to the men's. Why?

In the first place, Joan's theory has much greater scope than the men's. Whereas the geographical chart generates predictions for boiling temperatures only in a narrow band of territory, Joan's predicts boiling temperatures everywhere. But Joan's theory has still another advantage. It is more *elegant* than the other—that is, it makes a great number of predictions from a small number of statements. As scientists, any time we must choose between two laws or theories that generate identical predictions, we will opt for the more elegant one.

Elegance is one of our grounds for discarding Martin's animism and Calvin's teleology so readily. (Remember also that animism and teleology discourage scientific inquiry.) Martin, for example, might have devised a respectable law of boiling water. He might have said: "Whenever a hollow vessel containing water is put next to a fire, the fire god and the vessel god produce a child. This child causes the water to bubble violently and causes pain to anyone who touches its habitat." His prediction would have been the same as Isaac's: Water, when placed near fire, will bubble violently. However, the law is not elegant because it contains a number of terms unnecessary to the prediction. That these terms refer to variables incapable of observation is another strike against Martin.

THE PROBLEM OF HUMAN BEHAVIOR

Symbolic communication is a kind of behavior that probably is unique to human beings. Some people think that human behavior is not a suitable subject for scientific study. In the minds of these critics, human behavior is not determined in the same sense that physical phenomena are determined. Five such positions will be considered here. Adolf Grünbaum has analyzed four of them:

1. Human behavior is not amenable to causal description and therefore not predictable, since each individual is unique and not exactly like anyone else.

2. Even if there is a causal order in the phenomena of human behavior, it is so complex as to elude discovery permanently.

3. In the physical sciences, a present fact is always determined by past facts, but in human behavior present behavior is oriented toward future goals and thus "determined" by these future goals.

4. If human behavior were part of the causal order of events and thereby in principle predictable, it would be futile to attempt to make a choice between good and evil, meaningless to hold men responsible for their deeds, unjust to inflict punishment, and naïve to take seriously such remorse or guilt as is professed for past misdeeds. In short, the argument is that to assume the principle of causality in human behavior is incompatible with the known fact that people respond meaningfully to moral imperatives.[3]

If we are to feel secure in our scientific attempts to explain and predict communication behavior, we must frame replies to these propositions.

The first proposition, the argument from uniqueness, is the easiest to answer. The critics are right when they say that each individual is unique. They might even go farther and say that each behavior is unique—but so is each pot of boiling water and each air pump and each falling body unique. Every being and every event is unique, at least in space or in time. The hypotheses, laws, and theories of science functionally relate characteristics and activities of individuals, not the individuals themselves. In Isaac's studies, the heating and the boiling, not the water and the rock, were related by a law. Our own common sense observation belies the proposition that uniqueness of beings prohibits lawful behavior. Most of us would subscribe to the low-order law, "Infants, when moderately hungry, cry." This law does not deny the uniqueness of infants; it simply relates an antecedent state of those unique individuals, hunger, to a consequent state, crying. Although unique, the individuals are similar in a way that permits scientific generalization. When hungry, they cry.

We can answer the second proposition, the argument from complexity, in a similar way. The critics are right when they say that human behavior is complex. But so are all the natural phenomena to which science addresses itself complex; if they were not, science would be redundant. All of us could make all the predictions science makes with only the benefit of our own observations and inferences. We would have no need for the self-correcting process that science gives us. If the behavior of human beings is more complex than the behavior of the planets, we must simply try harder to understand it.

The third proposition, the argument from human purposiveness, gives the critics a stronger position but not an impregnable one. Science attempts to predict the future from the past, so the argument goes. However, in human behavior, such prediction is not possible, for human behavior is goal- (future) directed; therefore, the antecedent of behavior is something that has not yet occurred.

Answering this argument requires that we analyze, to some extent, the nature of human behavior. At first introspective glance, we are inclined to agree with the critics. Our present activities seem to be influenced by future events. A young executive's communications with his employer seem determined by the promotions he will get as a result of them.

When we pursue the thought, however, we notice that this analysis of our own behavior is oversimplified. Our behavior is not really determined by the future. It is determined partly by our *expectations* of the future and partly by our *perceptions* of the future. These expectations or perceptions are in the present, and they are suitable antecedents for predictions of consequent behavior. Our goals are not in the future, they are in the present. The outcomes to which our goal-directed behavior may lead are in the future, but these outcomes are by no means certain, nor is knowledge of them necessary to those sciences concerned with human behavior.

Of all the arguments marshaled by the critics, the fourth, the argument from freedom, is the most difficult to answer. If human behavior is amenable to scientific explanation, the argument goes, then human behavior is determined. It is a continuous chain of antecedents and their consequents. If that is so, then human behavior is not a function of will, of choice, or of freedom, and such notions as blame and guilt, praise and pride, are meaningless. If we cannot help what we are, then we should take neither credit nor discredit for our behavior. The answer to this argument is difficult to assimilate because it violates our own introspections. We all *know* that we have freedom, that we have exercised choice, and that we have experienced guilt for some activities and pride for others.

Our answer to this argument will be facilitated considerably if we can pretend for a few minutes that human behavior is determined—that each of our acts is a consequence of directly or indirectly observable antecedents. This position should not be difficult to take, for much of our experience leads us to it. Every time we make a prediction about another's behavior, we are taking, to some extent, a deterministic position. Certainly, we make many such predictions in our lifetime: "If I cry, Momma will feed me." "If I go to school late, the teacher will send me to the principal's office." "Dad's in a bad mood; if I ask for the car now, he won't let me have it." "If I just put transitions in this paper, the professor will give me a grade of A in the course." "If I show her the diamond when I propose, she will accept." "If I get Smith elected, he will lower the interest rate." "If I quit smoking, I will live longer." These predictions are based on deterministic assumptions. To the extent that we can make them and predictions like them accurately, we support a deterministic position. If human behavior were perfectly free, totally unconstrained by antecedents, it would be random, perfectly unpredictable.

If we can so readily accept a limited amount of determinism for human behavior, why do we rebel at the idea of going all the way? Why do we resist the notion that all our behavior is determined? Religious and egocentric arguments aside, the main obstacle is our own introspective experience. If we hurt another without provocation, we experience guilt. If we solve an especially difficult problem, we feel pride. We expect well-deserved punishment for the first action, well-deserved reward for the second.

The determinist's answer to this introspective paradox is to include guilt (an unpleasant feeling probably associated with the anticipation of punishment) and pride (a pleasant feeling probably associated with the anticipation of reward) as antecedent and consequent variables in his scheme for human behavior. People are born with the capacity to experience guilt and pride, he might say, and they learn the behavioral contexts in which these experiences are appropriate. Part of the antecedent condition determining behavior, therefore, is the anticipation of reward or punishment, of pride or guilt. Data is available on anticipation; therefore, this factor should enter into predictions about behavior and must be considered as a variable. However, the determinist's experience of choice, or what might be called his illusion of choice, should not be taken as evidence that his behavior is not predictable. His behavior's predictability or unpredictability is an empirical question that is open to scientific test. We cannot know whether scientific laws govern human behavior until we have made every attempt to discover them. We are only now beginning those attempts.

If we accept the determinist's position, we are left with two interesting questions: (1) Does the determinist himself experience guilt and pride? (2) Should society continue to punish those who violate its normative laws and reward those who are in some desirable way exceptional?

The answer to the first question is that the determinist probably would not label his postbehavior feelings with the nouns "guilt" or "pride." He might admit to feeling remorse about some past activity by saying, "I wish that I had done otherwise" or "I will do otherwise if similar circumstances occur." These statements mean that some alternative activity might have led to consequences that he now perceives as more desirable than the consequences of the activity he engaged in. He will not say, "I should have done otherwise" or even, "I could have done otherwise." He thinks that what he did was, at the time he did it, determined by antecedent variables, including himself and his past. He will explain the pleasurable feeling he has subsequent to other behaviors with the same rationale. He might say, "I'm glad I did that." This statement will result from the pleasurable consequences that he associates with his past behavior. He will not say, "I could have done otherwise."

The determinist's answer to the second question is, "It depends." Certainly, the anticipation of punishment inhibits some kinds of behavior and the anticipation of reward facilitates others. If society requires these anticipations of punishment and reward as antecedents to regulate behavior, then it should keep them. Administering punishment may enhance the inhibiting effect of the anticipation of further punishment. If it does, then punishment is one way of increasing control over behavior—punishment is a relevant antecedent. Possibly, says the determinist, other, more effective, relevant and controllable antecedents exist. The question is an empirical one. People probably should not be punished or rewarded except when the variables of reward and punishment are clearly relevant to their future behavior. Society seems to recognize this fact in its present attitude toward the insane and, to some extent, toward the poor.

The final argument against sciences of human behavior is

anticlimactic compared with the argument from freedom. B. F. Skinner relates the argument and his answer to it this way:

> Still another objection to the use of scientific method in the study of human behavior is that behavior is an anomalous subject matter because a prediction made about it may alter it. If we tell a friend that he is going to buy a particular kind of car, he may react to our prediction by buying a different kind. The same effect has been used to explain the failure of public opinion polls. In the presidential election of 1948 it was confidently predicted that a majority of the voters would vote for a candidate who, as it turned out, lost the election. It has been asserted that the electorate reacted to the prediction in a contrary way and that the published prediction therefore had an effect upon the predicted event. But it is by no means necessary that a prediction of behavior be permitted to affect the behaving individual. There may have been practical reasons why the results of the poll in question could not be withheld until after the election, but this would not be the case in a purely scientific endeavor.[4]

More anecdotal evidence can be added to Skinner's to make the case stronger for the proposition that predictions about behavior may alter it. One professor did a research project in which he tried to discover the effect of ordinal position on success in a speech contest. He studied the records of the Northern Oratorical League throughout its long history and discovered that the first speaker in the national contest had seldom been awarded a first-place judgment.[5] He published his results. The following year, the first speaker won the contest. In this case, as in the 1948 campaign, the availability of knowledge gathered by scientific processes may have affected the outcome of an event amenable to prediction from that knowledge.

Skinner's answer is that such knowledge need not necessarily be made available. This answer is unsatisfactory because it seems to advocate suppression of information, a practice repugnant to science.

A better answer, from a determinist's point of view, is that an individual's knowledge of predictions about his behavior should be considered simply as another antecedent for his behavior. In other words, his behavior should be predictable partly as a function of previous predictions known to him. And if the individual under study knows about the prediction that takes into account the earlier prediction, the determinist should be able to devise a third prediction using the first two as antecedents.

The preceding paragraphs should convince a student of communication that he is justified in pursuing the scientific study of symbol-using behavior even though such behavior may be uniquely human. Even if he does not accept the position that all human behavior is determined, his own experience must lead him to the conclusion that many fruitful generalizations are possible. For our purposes, that conclusion is sufficient.

GENERAL STATEMENT AND CONCLUSION

Science is a method of explaining events. Its aim is to enable accurate prediction of events. The method is not esoteric, nor does it depend on esoteric apparatus. Science is common sense made systematic and social.

Science depends on freely available information. It cannot exist where investigators are permitted to plead private knowledge or methods. To insure free access, science employs operationism, a method of description that enables complete, independent replication of observations and experiments. Given this openness in its method, science is self-correcting. Idiosyncratic errors in observation and inference are arrested early through independent validation. Scientific discovery requires publication so that inaccurate observations and unjustified inferences may be subject to the challenge of new observations and inferences.

Science typically proceeds through three mental stages. In the first stage, informal observation of facts leads to hypotheses —guesses about the relationships existing among these facts. (The origin of these initial guesses is a topic that needs study in the psychology of sciences.) In the second stage, these guesses are verified by further observation and achieve the status of laws—generalizations specifying the functional relationships among sets of facts. If the hypotheses are not verified, science requires that the process begin again, with new hypotheses. In the third stage, science attempts theory—generalizations broader in scope than laws that express functional relationships among facts previously unrelated by laws. At all three stages, speculation interacts with observation. Moreover, all three kinds of statements, from hypothesis to theory, must have built into them predictions that could lead to their own abandonment. A "hypothesis" or "law" or "theory" that can be conciliated with *any* contingency is not scientific, even though its grammatical form may make it look scientific. Scientists must specify the facts that, if observed, will force them to modify or abandon their own statements.

An appropriate end to this chapter is a return to its beginning and a final comment about apparatus and scientists. Although instrumentation is not essential to science, it sometimes permits new precision in old generalizations (as with Gordon's thermometer) and occasionally makes possible verification of previously unverifiable hypotheses. Part of a paragraph from a perceptive historian and philosopher of science, Edwin G. Boring, makes this point clear:

> *Advance in knowledge is rapid when new methods or new instruments become available.* The building of telescopes in 1608 led to Galileo's constructing his in 1609 and his discovery of four of Jupiter's moons. That discovery upset theologically tempered science by showing that the Creator had exceeded the sacred number seven in his making of the celestial bodies, and later it provided the means for the measurement of the velocity of light. . . . Volta's invention of the battery, the invention of electromagnets and of the galvanometer, all in the early nineteenth century, made possible the study and measurement of the nerve impulse by du Bois-Reymond in the middle of the century and the invention of many other electrical instruments, like the chronograph and the chronoscope. The astronomers could measure absolute reaction times when they had these electrical devices. Similarly in the present century the devel-

opment of the electronic tube has revolutionized, not only psychoacoustics, but also all sorts of laboratory work in physics, physiology, and psychology.[6]

As Boring says, the point is obvious.

The earlier illustrations should also have made the point that scientists share the weaknesses of other human beings. Interpersonal relationships enter into the interpretation of data and the acceptance of laws and theories. Although the public nature of science insures the eventual detection of error, it does not assure a machinelike precision in building and altering laws and theories. We can detect systematically the debilitating effect of at least three of these human foibles.

Scientists tend not to discard a theory, even in the face of contradictory facts, until it is replaced by a better theory. This reluctance is not unique to scientists. As human beings, we like to generalize. In spite of their dangers of oversimplification and inaccuracy, generalizations make us efficient. The only substitute for a generalization is a catalog of facts, and we dislike remembering catalogs even if we have exceptional memories. Therefore, despite their faults, we keep our generalizations until more accurate generalizations come along. James Conant expresses this weakness as it applies to science: "A conceptual scheme is never discarded merely because of a few stubborn facts with which it cannot be reconciled; a conceptual scheme is either modified or replaced by a better one, never abandoned with nothing left to take its place." [7]

Another weakness that scientists bring to science is their tendency to hold some individuals in high esteem. Scientists sometimes hesitate to discard the theories of a prestigious theorist during his lifetime, even when they are confronted with contrary evidence. Edwin Boring writes that "Many commentators have remarked at the difficulty with which scientists abandon a theory, once important but now outmoded, until its author dies, for the author's prestige may maintain the authority of the Great Man even in the face of contradictory evidence." [8]

Finally, the personality and interpersonal relationships of the theorist might adversely affect the acceptance of his theory. Again, we can take our evidence from Boring. He relates the account of how Mesmer, an "egotistic, opinionated" person, discovered hypnotism for science and how his discovery was rejected by scientists in the eighteenth century. Mesmer's activities were completely observable. His explanations were, at the time, scientifically respectable. He even found a Swiss priest who was also practicing hypnotism as medical treatment. Mesmer himself was a physician. He had the credentials for making credible discoveries; yet his discoveries were rejected for about two centuries. Even 60 years later a British physician, also a rather aggressive man, was castigated for using hypnotism as an anesthetic. Boring summarizes his interpretation of the case:

> . . . if science is, as is so often claimed, quite impersonal, Mesmer's personality ought to have nothing to do with the question of his demonstration of the truth of animal magnetism [hypnotism]. Nobody knows whether Mesmer in young manhood was more conceited than the average of men who later become famous. It is quite clear, however, that, even had he been a modest and retiring person when young, his great theory that an important beneficent power resided in his own person would have made him into the sort of man that his opponents would regard as vain. In fact, conceit was involved in his scientific theory, since the theory had to do specifically with Mesmer. Yet nobody in the various investigating committees or in the Académie des Sciences was objective enough to see this crucial point. They denounced Mesmer, largely, so it seems to me, because of his personality, and thus mingled their own personalities with their scientific criticism.[9]

From this discussion, a picture of science as a method to safeguard accuracy of observations and to encourage scope in predictive generalizations should have emerged. Instruments and specific individuals may accelerate the progress of science but its essence is method. Scientists share common human failings, but their point of view as scientists should minimize those failings when the aim is predictive explanation.

Notes

1. This chapter owes much to lectures by Professor Gustav Bergmann and to Herbert Feigl, "Naturalism and Humanism," *American Quarterly*, I (1949), 139–142.

2. For an excellent discussion of this relationship, see Fred N. Kerlinger, *Foundations of Behavioral Research* (New York: Holt, Rinehart and Winston, 1967), pp. 3–17.

3. Adolf Grünbaum, "Causality and the Science of Human Behavior," *American Scientist*, XL (1952), 667. Reprinted in Herbert Feigl and May Brodbeck (eds.), *Readings in the Philosophy of Science* (New York: Appleton-Century-Crofts, 1953), p. 768.

4. B. F. Skinner, *Science and Human Behavior* (New York: Macmillan, 1953), pp. 20–21.

5. Sam L. Becker, "The Ordinal Position Effect," *Quarterly Journal of Speech*, XXXIX (1953), 217–219.

6. Edwin G. Boring, "Great Men and Scientific Progress," *Proceedings of the American Philosophical Society*, XCIV (1950), 342. Reprinted in Edwin G. Boring, *History, Psychology, and Science* (New York: Wiley, 1963), p. 35.

7. James B. Conant, *Science and Common Sense* (New Haven, Conn.: Yale University Press, 1951), p. 173.

8. Edwin G. Boring, "Eponym as Placebo," in *History, Psychology, and Science*, p. 8.

9. Edwin G. Boring, "The Psychology of Controversy," *Psychological Review*, XXXVI (1929), 99–100. Reprinted in *History, Psychology, and Science*, p. 69.

2

Designing the Communication Experiment

As pointed out in Chapter One, people experiment with communication much of the time. Consider the following classic short dialogue:

MOTHER   Johnny, eat your spinach.

JOHNNY   I don't like it.

MOTHER   You need spinach to get big and strong. (*Johnny does not respond.*)

MOTHER   Don't you want to grow up to be like daddy? Look, he's eating his.

JOHNNY   I don't like it, mother.

MOTHER   Spinach is good food for your bones. You could get really sick without spinach. (*Johnny does not respond.*)

MOTHER   It tastes good, Johnny. Just try it. You'll like it.

JOHNNY   (smelling the spinach)   I can't eat it.

MOTHER If you just take one bite, I'll give you a piece of candy after supper.

JOHNNY I can't.

MOTHER If you don't at least try it, you can't have any dessert.

(*Johnny does not respond.*)

The mother clearly is experimenting with communication in an attempt to exercise social control. She manipulates a number of independent variables in order to change the state of one dependent variable, Johnny's behavior with his spinach. At least eight such independent variables can be detected:

1. The mother's first response to the situation, a simple request, is an exercise of what might be called her referent power. She knows that Johnny sometimes does things that he otherwise wouldn't do simply because she asks him to.

2. In her second response, she holds out to Johnny the distant reward of good health. She assumes that this is one of his goals, and she makes it salient for him by relating it to the spinach.

3. When manipulation of this variable fails, she attaches to it what she thinks might be a stronger motive for Johnny, identification with his father. If Johnny has brothers or sisters, she might also at this point employ a little sibling rivalry by saying, "Look, even Julie eats her spinach."

4. Apparently, exercises of power and promises of remote, abstract rewards fail as independent variables. In her fourth response, the mother resorts to anticipation of remote punishment, the possibility of a mysterious bone disease.

5. Next, the mother tries the promise of immediate pleasure, the good taste of the spinach. Here, Johnny does a little testing of his own. The smell of the spinach, to him at least, belies his mother's promise. He prefers to base his action on the physical reality of the smell rather than the social reality of his mother's promise.

6. The mother knows that Johnny likes candy. Her social reality corresponds with his physical reality, so she tries to use anticipation of receiving candy as a relatively immediate reward.

7. When the promise of immediate reward fails, the mother resorts to anticipation of immediate deprivation (no spinach, no dessert).

8. Finally, the mother might perceive the very length of the dialogue as a relevant independent variable. If Johnny finally does eat his spinach, she probably will undertake a similarly long exchange on the next such occasion, possibly with broccoli.

The mother clearly is employing a method that is closely akin to the experimental method of science. Although her control over the conditions of the experiment may not be ideal and although any law she derives from her research will be narrow in scope, the case does serve as an introduction to experimental design.

THE BASIC DESIGN

John Stuart Mill systematized the thought from which the basic experimental design comes.[1] This thought can be reduced to the following proposition: *If a variable known to be a consequent occurs when a variable thought to be an antecedent has preceded it but does not occur, other things being constant, when the variable thought to be an antecedent has not preceded it, then a causal relationship can be said to exist between the antecedent variable and the consequent variable.* Earlier in this book, the consequent variable was labeled the dependent variable and the suspected antecedent variables were labeled the independent variables. The condition requiring that the suspected antecedent variable be present is called the experimental condition; the condition requiring that it be absent is called the control condition. Abstractly, these conditions can be represented in a successful experiment as follows:

(Experimental condition) If A, then B.
(Control condition)   If non-A, then non-B.

In this abstraction, B is the consequent variable, A the suspected antecedent variable.

To represent this method of thought concretely, the example of Isaac and the boiling water can be used as well as any other. In that series of experiments, Isaac was concerned with one dependent variable (the boiling of the water) and four independent variables (the vessel, the fire, the water, the nearness to the fire). His first experiment went like this:

(Experimental condition) If $water_1$ then boiling.
                            $fire_1$
                            $vessel_1$
                            nearness to $fire_1$

(Control condition)   If $water_1$ then no boiling.
                            $fire_1$
                            $vessel_1$
                            no nearness to $fire_1$

From this experiment, Isaac could assert that a causal relationship existed between boiling and nearness to fire for this particular set of variables.

Isaac was not satisfied with the restricted generality of this relationship. He therefore conducted a second experiment in an attempt to increase the scope of the asserted relationship:

(Experimental condition) If $water_2$ then boiling.
                            $fire_1$
                            $vessel_2$
                            nearness to $fire_1$

For this experiment, Isaac perceived the nonagitation of the water in $rock_2$ before he placed it near the fire as being an adequate control. Also, he saw the control condition in his first experiment as being relevant to this experiment.

So far, the only independent variable for which Isaac did not have a control was $fire_1$. He therefore built another fire and simultaneously set up two other experimental conditions:

(Experimental condition) If water$_3$ then boiling.
                           fire$_2$
                           vessel$_3$
                           nearness to fire$_2$

(Experimental condition) If water$_4$ then boiling.
                           fire$_2$
                           vessel$_4$
                           nearness to fire$_2$

Isaac furnished at least one control condition for each of the independent variables that he perceived as possibly relevant to the boiling. He therefore published his law with some confidence, asserting a functional relationship between nearness to fire and boiling. Water boiled whenever it was near any of the fires in Isaac's experiments. Furthermore, it did not boil, as far as Isaac could tell in his systematic investigation, under any other conditions. Until someone uses facts to alter his law, then, Isaac will operate under the assumption that water boils when it is near fire but not otherwise.

As will be shown later, contemporary communication research often employs experimental designs that are much more complex than this one, though they are no different in principle. For the moment, however, only one inadequacy in this basic design need be noted. The design proceeds from an all-or-nothing assumption, a premise that a variable is either present or absent. Contemporary science, including social science, often requires more precise quantification than the simple observation that something is either present or absent. Therefore, the basic experimental design is often considered one by means of which corresponding differences are detected in the *quantities* of dependent variables as functions of differences in the *quantities* of independent variables. This method is called *concomitant variation*. Such a method can be represented abstractly with the following statements:

(Control condition)   If non-A, then non-B.
(Experimental condition) If a little A, then a little B.
(Experimental condition) If more A, then more B.
(Experimental condition) If medium A, then medium B.
(Experimental condition) If much A, then much B.

This design probably requires no further explanation. Its underlying principle is exactly the same as that of the basic design. The only refinement is that either variable can be measured in quantities other than zero (absent) and one (present).

THE PROBLEM OF CHANCE FLUCTUATION

Designing and analyzing experiments in communication is not quite as straightforward as this discussion of the basic design might imply. Perhaps the major problem is our realization of the fact that we cannot ascribe all variations in our dependent variable to variations in our independent variable because our laws are far from perfect. Many of the variables that we do not or cannot control may be functionally related to the variables we define as dependent. Thus, we expect some variation in the dependent variable from experiment to experiment as the result of influences other than those emanating from the independent variables we succeed in controlling. All the variation resulting from uncontrolled variables is commonly lumped together and called *chance fluctuation* in the dependent variable. An illustration will be useful.

As experimentalists in communication, we might be interested in the question: Does the presence of other people facilitate vocalization in very young (prelanguage) children? We design an experiment to test for a functional relationship between presence of others and vocalization.

For this experiment we direct our attention specifically to the mother as a facilitator of vocalization in young children. Our hypothesis is a simple one: Vocalization by prelanguage children is greater in the presence of the mother than in her absence.

Now we must operationalize the variables referred to in the hypothesis. To this end, we solicit the cooperation of two families that we consider normal, each of which has an eight-month-old child. The two children, Jeanne and Tommy, become our experimental subjects.

Next, we must devise a measure of "vocalization." We have a number of options available. For example, we might count the number of detectable syllables the child utters, or we might measure in seconds the output generated by a voice-activated microphone. If we accepted the second alternative, we would even have to count crying as "vocalization." We finally decide that the best measure, for our interests, would be time in seconds of noncrying vocalization. If we encounter instances on the tape recordings where we cannot decide whether a vocalization is "crying" or "noncrying," we will refer the decision to the mother.

The independent variable, presence or absence of the mother, is easy to manipulate, given her cooperation. However, we face the problem of controlling other possibly relevant variables. We would like to make our tests as natural as possible. A strange environment may affect the vocalization of one child differently from the way it affects the vocalization of the other. Therefore, we decide to conduct our experiment in the subjects' homes. The time variable is also obviously relevant. We discover from the mothers that their children are normally awake simultaneously between 11 A.M. and noon. We decide to conduct our tests between 11:00 and 11:30. We also note that family patterns of behavior may produce more vocalization on some days of the week than on others. Because we obviously cannot control family patterns of behavior, we decide to design our experiment in such a way that both levels of the independent variable ("alone" and "with mother") occur at least once during each day of the week. We can then feel safe in assuming that whatever irregularities occur because of the day-of-week variable affects both conditions equally. If we want to be even more sophisticated, we can analyze the data in such a way that whatever effects the day-of-week variable might have are extracted from the test of our more critical alone-or-with-mother variable. Finally, we recognize that eight-month-old babies sometimes cry for inordinately long periods. When babies are crying, they cannot be vocalizing normally. Therefore, we decide to adjust the measure of the dependent variable (sometimes called the criterion measure) to allow for crying behavior. We can make this adjustment by using a ratio of seconds spent vocalizing to seconds of noncrying behavior (vocal and quiet) in each of our half-hour periods. For example, if on a given day, Tommy cried for 3 minutes, vocalized for 8 minutes, and did not vocalize for the remaining 19 minutes of his half-hour period, we would calculate his "score" for that day as follows: 1,800 seconds (time of the test) minus 180 seconds (time crying) equals 1,620 seconds (noncrying behavior). 480 seconds (time vocalizing) divided by 1,620 seconds (noncrying behavior) equals .296. This last number, .296, is the ratio of Tommy's vocalizing behavior to all of his noncrying behavior during the test period that day. In effect, using this ratio makes Tommy's crying behavior irrelevant to the analysis. Crying neither helps nor hurts his vocalizing score.

We now give our final instructions. We have decided to run our tests over two weeks, because during that period we can have each child in the "alone" and the "with-mother" condition on each day of the week. We tell each mother what her schedule is and inform her that all tests are to occur in the same room of the house at the same time of the day. During the "with-mother" condition, the mother is simply to sit where the child can see her, but she is not to respond to anything the child does or says, either vocally or nonvocally. She is to read a book, knit, or engage in some similar activity. Our tape recorders are installed; the playpens are ready for occupancy.

As a result of our measurements and calculations, we arrive at the scores shown in Table 1.

Now our problem is to make sense from the data. When we first glance at the table, we notice hopefully that in many cases each child's "with-mother" score is higher than the "alone" score, but we do not want to report that a subjective glance reveals a real difference between the two conditions. Somehow, we must summarize the data.

One way to condense the data is simply to add up all the "alone" scores for the two children and all the "with-mother" scores. Because we observed the children in each of the two

TABLE 1   Vocalization Ratios for Two Children "Alone" and "With Mother" *

	Tommy		Jeanne	
Day of Week	Alone	With Mother	Alone	With Mother
Sunday 1	.328			.550
Monday 1		.462	.536	
Tuesday 1	.228			.699
Wednesday 1		.284	.640	
Thursday 1	.418			.584
Friday 1		.349	.414	
Saturday 1	.475			.640
Sunday 2		.374	.622	
Monday 2	.324			.451
Tuesday 2		.500	.426	
Wednesday 2	.237			.692
Thursday 2		.263	.685	
Friday 2	.310			.475
Saturday 2		.382	.494	

* Hypothetical data.

conditions the same number of times, the two sums should be comparable. When we perform that calculation, we notice that the "with-mother" sum is higher, as we had hypothesized:

"Alone" sum	6.137
"With-mother" sum	6.705

This difference makes us think that we might be on our way to confirming a hypothesis. But we would like to talk about the difference in terms other than sums. We think a comparison of the average vocalization ratio "alone" with the average vocalization ratio "with mother" would be desirable so that we could say: "On an ordinary day, the 'alone' ratio is X, the 'with-mother' ratio, Y." To find this average, we divide each of

the sums by the number of observations it represents (14).
We find:

| "Alone" average | .438 |
| "With-mother" average | .479 |

We still are not confident that the difference we found represents a functional relationship between our experimental conditions and amount of vocalization. We know that many uncontrolled variables might have affected the children's output, even though we did our best to keep constant the obvious ones. One child's father might have left for work late one day, exciting baby and mother and increasing the baby's production. One child might have had a restless night, depressing his production the following day. These random, chance variables might have affected our data at least as much as our independent variable did. We would like to give ourselves some assurance that the difference we found is not easily attributable to such random antecedents.

The formal statistical techniques available to test the operation of chance in an experiment of this kind will not be discussed here, for such descriptions are easily available elsewhere. However, this illustration can be used as a basis for the discussion of many of these techniques.

We reason that if our experimental conditions are functionally related to amount of vocalization, then the superiority of the "with-mother" condition should be consistent—that is, during a major proportion of the time, the children should produce more vocalization in the "with-mother" than in the "alone" condition. Thus, if we chart our data, we should find the "with-mother" ratios clustered at one end and the "alone" ratios clustered at the other. This clustering does not occur in Figure 2, where *A* stands for "alone" and *M* stands for "with mother."

At this point, our hypothesis does not appear to be tenable. As Figure 2 shows, the two distributions have much more space in common than separately. The entire range of scores covers 471 units (the highest score, .699, minus the lowest score, .228).

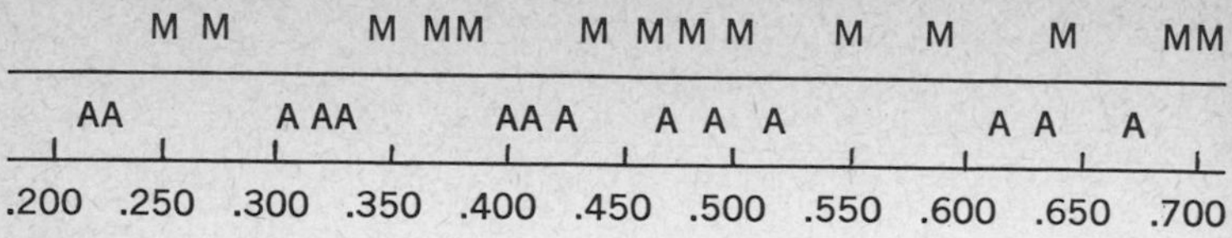

Figure 2 Distribution of Vocalization Ratios
"Alone" and "With Mother"

Of this range, only 48 units are not shared by the two distributions. We therefore must conclude that the differences we found between the "alone" condition and the "with-mother" condition could easily have occurred as the result of chance variables, rather than as the result of the variable we manipulated.

What would the data in Table 1 have looked like when distributed in a figure if the hypothesis tested had been different? We can consider the scores of the two children from another point of view to find out.

A second inspection of Table 1 indicates that a strong difference might exist between the production ratios of Tommy and Jeanne. We did not predict this difference; thus any analysis of it cannot result in a law. However, pursuing this analysis might give us some informative hints for future studies. We will proceed in exactly the manner we used to analyze the "alone" and "with-mother" difference.

First we will add up all the "Tommy" scores and all the "Jeanne" scores. Again, because we observed each child the same number of times, the two sums should be comparable:

Tommy sum   4.934
Jeanne sum   7.908

Jeanne's sum is more different from Tommy's than the "with-mother" sum was different from the "alone" sum.

An average might make more sense to us than a sum. Again, we would like to be able to think of each child's vocalization on a typical day. Therefore, we calculate an average by dividing each of the sums by the number of observations it represents (14).

Tommy average .352
Jeanne average .564

Because the totals differed more than in the previous study, the averages do also, of course.

However, we recall that these two indications of differences are not very informative, for they tell us nothing about the distribution of the scores for the two children. If the two distributions overlap to a great extent, we will be inclined to distrust the apparent differences represented in the totals and averages. In largely overlapping distributions, these apparent differences could easily be attributable to uncontrolled, random variables. They might simply be an indication of chance fluctuation.

If we had predicted a difference between Jeanne and Tommy rather than between the "alone" condition and the "with-mother" condition, the distributions represented in Figure 3

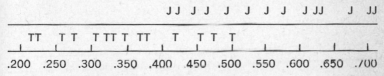

Figure 3 Distribution of Vocalization Ratios
for Tommy and Jeanne

would give us great satisfaction. Jeanne's superior output is strongly consistent. In the range of 471 units, the two distributions overlap in a relatively narrow band, 86 units (Tommy's highest score, .500, minus Jeanne's lowest score, .414). We can feel quite confident that the two children's vocalization ratios differ as the result of something other than random variables.

Statisticians have worked out a technique called analysis of variance, by which an experimenter can calculate with some precision the probability that a difference between two averages is the result of uncontrolled, chance variables. This method is analogous to the informal charting of distributions just discussed and compares variation *within* experimental groups to variation *among* such groups. If the variation among groups is much greater than the variation within groups, then the experimenter can assume that the difference he has found is a real one, rather than an apparent one resulting from chance fluctuations. Typically he reports from the statistics the degree of probability with which he can buttress his confidence in the statement that his differences are real. Thus, in the published report of almost every communication experiment can be found phrases like .05 level of significance, 95 percent level of confidence, p (probability) $< .05$. All of these phrases mean the same thing: The probability that the difference found would occur as the result of chance fluctuation is less than 5 percent, or 1 in 20. Most social scientists, including experimenters in communication, will accept as real any difference reaching this .05 level of significance; most will not accept as real any difference not reaching this level.

THE PROBLEM OF RANDOM SELECTION

We do not need a psychologist to tell us that at this stage in the development of behavioral science, most of the behavior of most people is not predictable from scientific laws or theories. This statement is especially true of communication behavior. Communication scientists can predict the effects of a few variables on a few other variables in a few contexts. Mostly, however, they are still in the dark.

A whole cluster of variables not yet comprehended and therefore not yet amenable to control is associated with individual differences. If, for example, a teacher says to his class of 15 students, "Conduct a communication experiment," he is likely to get 15 different responses. He might be able to predict a few of these responses, but most of them will have at least some element of surprise.

These individual differences make the communication scholar's attempts to establish lawful relationships especially difficult. He may achieve considerable success in making predictions for one individual (in a therapy situation, for example). But his aim is to formulate laws that relate large classes of behaviors to other large classes—that is, he wants to be able to generalize.

Generalizing in the social sciences almost always requires sampling. The communication scholar selects a group of people, performs tests with that group, and attempts to extend his results to people in general. He calls the group with which he works a sample; he calls the group to which he extends his findings a population. His major problem is to see that his sample is representative of the population about which he hopes to generalize.

The necessity for sampling in communication science arises from the fact that communication characteristics differ from one person to another. If all persons were exactly alike in their communicative behavior, sampling would be unnecessary, for any law applying to one individual would apply to all others. Because of this variability, scientists concerned with physical laws have an advantage over scientists attempting to discover psychological and social laws. Isaac, for example, could assume that one fire was basically like any other fire and that one pot of water was similar to any other as far as the characteristics he was interested in were concerned. People studying communication usually cannot make such assumptions, although students of some characteristics encounter lower variability than students of others. Linguists, for example, frequently assume that almost all individuals from the same socioeconomic class who are reared in the same region will have similar dialectal and lexical characteristics.

Given the varied nature of human communication characteristics, how can a communication scholar be assured that his samples are representative and that generalization is justified? In other words, how can the communication scholar avoid bias in his samples? Most scholars attempt to solve this problem by random sampling, which requires that every entity in the population have an equal chance of appearing in the sample. It can be shown, both mathematically and empirically, that a sample so chosen, given sufficient size, almost certainly involves no gross biases.

To illustrate, suppose that we are interested in whatever laws are to be found governing the slang used by American college students. We suspect that slang terms are more likely to refer to some kinds of things than to other kinds of things. As a general hypothesis, we predict that slang terms are likely to be invented to refer to things, people, and events that are important to American college students as a group. As a step toward making this hypothesis operational, we draw up a list of such entities:

1. Positive references to peer group members of the opposite sex
2. Negative references to peer group members of the opposite sex
3. References to studying just before an examination
4. References to parents
5. Positive references to professors and the courses they teach
6. Negative references to professors and the courses they teach
7. References to prominent, identifiable social groups
8. Positive references to performances on examinations and in courses
9. Negative references to performances on examinations and in courses
10. References to sexual behavior
11. General positive references
12. General negative references

An informal poll of classmates reveals that they do have slang terms for entities in each of the 12 categories.

Now we are ready for the more interesting part of our study. We would like to discover laws governing the formation of slang terms. Examination of our informal poll leads us to the following specific hypotheses:

1. Evaluative references to peer group members of the opposite sex are likely to be animal analogies.

2. References to studying before an examination are likely to involve space-filling analogies.
3. References to parents are likely to contain mention of nurturing.
4. Evaluative references to professors and the courses they teach are likely to be one-syllable nonsense words whose final phoneme is a plosive.
5. References to prominent and identifiable social groups are likely to be in the form of acronyms or abbreviations of the official names of those groups, sometimes including an evaluative animal analogy.
6. Evaluative references to performances on examinations and in courses are likely to be nonsense expansions of the grade "A" and the grade "F."
7. References to sexual behavior are likely to be transitive, one-syllable verbs whose final phoneme is a plosive.
8. General evaluative references are likely to involve temperature analogies.

Confirmation of these hypotheses could lead to relatively respectable semantic laws that relate symbols to their referents. We decide to proceed by carefully constructing a questionnaire designed to elicit slang terms from college respondents. The questionnaire contains items like the following:

> You are in a required course that seems to you to serve no useful purpose. The content is dull and the professor's manner of presenting it is duller. The examinations seem to you unfair and trivial. The professor is uninterested in his subject and in his students. With this in mind, please respond to the following items:
>
> In conversations with close friends, I would call the course a(n) —————.
>
> In conversations with close friends, I would call the professor a(n) —————.

Having already decided that we would like to generalize to college students in the United States, our problem now is to select a sample. Our first impulse is to administer the questionnaire to our close friends, those people most readily available to us. A moment's thought, however, tells us that such a sample would obviously be biased because our friends are probably different in many respects from the population of United States college students. We therefore discard this plan.

One member of our research group, who is also a member of a national fraternity, claims that without much difficulty he could have the questionnaire administered to the members of his fraternity on campuses throughout the country. However, we recognize immediately that this plan also introduces bias to the sample, though it reduces geographical bias. We suspect that fraternity members as a group may employ slang in a way different from the way slang is employed by the population of all students in the United States. Furthermore, slang on campuses that have a Greek system may be systematically different from slang on campuses that have none.

To have a perfectly random sample, we would have to acquire student directories from each of the approximately 2,500 colleges and universities in the United States. Then we would have to assign a number to each name in all the directories and draw at random as many numbers as we intended to include in our sample. Finally, we would have to administer the questionnaire to those individuals whose numbers were drawn. We decide that this procedure would be impractical.

A possibility occurs to us that would increase the yield of information from our study and simplify this information as well. We decide to think of the population of American undergraduates as a set of subpopulations, defined on some basis that might make a difference in the use of slang. Two such bases might be geographical distribution and prestige of the institution. We therefore stratify our sample operationally and select a quota of students from various institutions representing differences in region and prestige. Several ways of making such decisions come to mind. We might select for study a school from the Ivy League, one from the Big Ten, one from the Southeastern Conference, one from the Southwestern Conference, one from the Pacific Coast Conference, and several community colleges distributed across the country. Given a sample of schools randomly selected from strata identified on some such basis, we would then randomly select samples of students from the schools. This procedure would include the theoretical and empirical advantages of a random sample as well as two additional grounds (geography and prestige) for analysis of the data. Because our grounds for selection of institutions are open to inspection, any bias in our sample could be checked by further study. Such a procedure is called stratified random sampling.

MORE COMPLEX DESIGNS

So far, the discussion has focused on the simple experimental design, in which two conditions are employed: (1) the experimental condition, in which the independent variable is present, and (2) the control condition, in which all variables governing the experimental condition except the independent variable are present.

Most contemporary communication experiments make use of more efficient designs that simultaneously employ more than one set of independent variables and often use more than one set of dependent variables. Often, such designs have no control condition as defined above—every subject is exposed to some combination of experimental variables under the assumption that each condition serves as a control, a point of comparison, for all the others.

Suppose that as communication scholars we are concerned with the problem of recruiting volunteers, especially males, for experiments. This problem is a real one for many social scientists for two reasons: (1) volunteers are simply hard to obtain, and (2) unless everybody in a potential sample volunteers, those who do cannot be considered a random sample. We see in the problem a chance to do research that might have practical as well as theoretical value.

One member of our research group, a young graduate student, has an extremely attractive, intelligent, socially adept, nineteen-year-old sister who is a sophomore at the same university. In a brainstorming session about the volunteer problem, he says, "I'll bet almost any unmarried male in school would volunteer to be a subject if he were offered a dinner date with Judy." This statement is enough to prompt a series of experiments.

Because our department has a standing policy of permitting appeals for volunteers in all its classes and because we offer courses required of all students at all levels, getting a representative sample of subjects for our studies is no problem. Before we can proceed, however, we must compose our experimental messages.

The standard message we have been using in such appeals is as follows:

> As all of you know, this is a research as well as teaching department. We try to discover new knowledge about communication as well as to teach what we already know. Very often, research in communication requires human subjects for experimental work.
>
> Because this university has a policy against requiring students to participate in experiments, we must depend on volunteers whenever we cannot afford to pay experimental subjects. As you all know, graduate students are notoriously poor and seldom have money to pay subjects for participating in thesis and dissertation research.
>
> We hope that you will want to help add to the store of knowledge available to future generations of students, just as former students have added to the store of knowledge available to you. We are now going to pass around an "Experimental Volunteer Sign-up Sheet." If you sign, you will be committing one hour of your time to this valuable work.

We decide to use this message as the persuasive appeal in our control condition.

For the experimental condition, we use exactly the same message except that we add the following paragraph between the middle and last paragraphs:

> This semester, we are offering an added inducement for male volunteers. We will put the name of every male student who

volunteers in a lottery. In about a month, when all the experiments are completed, we will draw the name of one of these volunteers and will fully support him financially for a dinner date with Judy, seated here on the right, at a local night club.

This study, of course, is an example of the simple experimental design. The independent variable, the paragraph referring to Judy, is present in the experimental condition but absent in the control condition. The dependent variable is the proportion of male students who volunteer for experimental work. According to the reasoning discussed earlier, any difference greater than that to be expected by chance should be attributable to the paragraph referring to Judy, assuming random assignment of subjects to groups.

To meet the randomness requirement, we select without bias six sections of students enrolled in our large freshman course. We arrange for our speaker, the young graduate student, to appear in all six sections at the beginning of the class period for each section. (The same speaker is used in all six sections so that any differential effects cannot be attributed to appearance or delivery variables.) Although no reference is made to Judy in the control sections, we require her smiling and charming presence in case it makes a difference regardless of the experimental paragraph in the appeal.

To make our analysis easier, we randomly discard the subjects from some sections until we have an equal number, 20, in each. The results of this procedure appear in Table 2.

A glance at the tables shows us that our manipulations failed to produce the desired result. Even the participation of the class with the highest proportion of volunteers reached only 50 percent. Obviously, some sort of selectivity was operating, and we cannot consider this group of volunteers to be a random sample.

To give us a visual check on the reliability of whatever differences do appear between the experimental and control conditions, we arrange the data to show overlap (see Figure 4) and find that the two distributions overlap substantially. Therefore, any apparent differences could be the result of random

TABLE 2 Number and Percentage of Sign-ups "With Judy Paragraph" and "Without Judy Paragraph" *

Class	With Judy Paragraph		Without Judy Paragraph	
	Number	Percent	Number	Percent
A	4	20		
B			5	25
C	7	35		
D			6	30
E	9	45		
F			10	50

* Hypothetical data.

variables, and we can attribute no effects to the experimental manipulation.

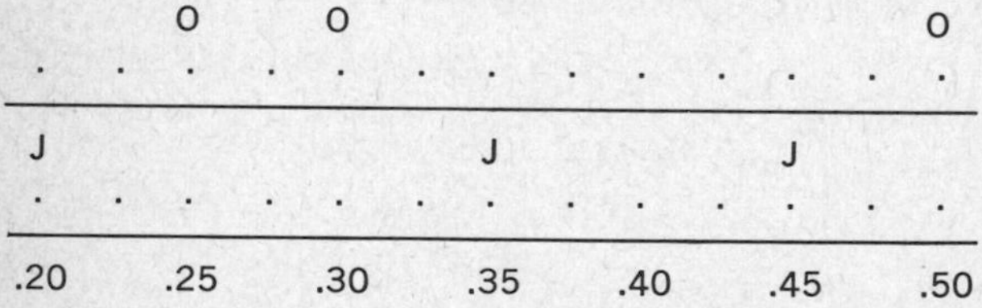

Figure 4 Distribution of Proportions for "Judy" (J) and "No-Judy" (O) Conditions

Our study now begins to attract the attention of others in our department. When we meet to discuss the results, a senior member of the faculty gives a short speech:

I've had experience with quite a lot of work on persuasion, and unexpected results seem to be the norm. I've evolved a way of thinking about the process that might be helpful.

Now, our first impulse is to consider persuasion as a very simple process. We think that if we appeal to a motive we know to exist, our persuasion will automatically be successful.

And we know that those young men in those classes would like to have a date with Judy. We'd like to have one ourselves. Yet, they didn't sign up as volunteers.

This situation indicates to me that we're thinking about persuasion in the wrong way. I think that in almost every case of persuasion various forces are working—some facilitating action, others inhibiting it. Clearly, the prospect of having this date with Judy facilitates action. But something else in the situation must inhibit it just as strongly.

My hypothesis is that freshman men, in general, have very fragile self-esteem. For that reason, they hate to admit weakness. But consider the situation you put them in. You ask them, in front of their peers of both sexes, to take a chance on getting a date. They perceive failure in this attempt as a threat to their self-esteem. If they sign up, they see themselves as admitting, both to themselves and to their peers, that they can't get dates for themselves with girls as attractive as Judy. They have to depend on a lottery. This thought obviously inhibits them from volunteering. I'm surprised you got as many volunteers from the experimental classes as you did.

To check my interpretation, I suggest that you do a second study in which you control two variables instead of only one. Seniors, I think, won't show this self-esteem effect. Judy's attractiveness will facilitate persuasion as much with them as with the freshmen, but the inhibiting effect of self-esteem won't be nearly so strong for the seniors. So I think you should do the same study, this time using both senior classes and freshman classes.

We decide to take the professor's advice. The experimental design is shown in Figure 5. We refer to a design like this in general as an "$A \times B$ design," A standing for one variable, B for the other.

	With Judy Paragraph	Without Judy Paragraph
Freshmen	3 classes	3 classes
Seniors	3 classes	3 classes

Figure 5 A X B Design

This experimental design has more advantages over the simple design than we might at first suppose. We could consider it simply as two simple designs incorporated into the same experiment. This point of view would lead us to consider the effects of maturity (seniors versus freshmen) and motive appeal ("with Judy paragraph" versus "without Judy paragraph") separately. But in this experiment we are interested in more than that. We are looking for the way in which the two variables affect each other—that is, we are looking for *interaction*. We hypothesize that the maturity variable, by itself, will have only a slight effect and that the motive appeal variable, by itself, will have only a slight effect. However, we predict that when maturity is combined with the motive appeal, the effect will be much stronger. To test the hypothesis, we follow exactly the same procedures as we did in the first simple experi-

TABLE 3 Number and Percentage of Sign-ups "With Judy Paragraph" and "Without Judy Paragraph" Among Freshmen and Seniors*

Class	With Judy Paragraph		Without Judy Paragraph	
	Number	Percent	Number	Percent
Freshmen				
A	10	50		
B			7	35
C	5	25		
D			9	45
E	6	30		
F			4	20
Seniors				
G	16	80		
H			4	20
I	19	95		
J			3	15
K	17	85		
L			5	25

* Hypothetical data.

ment. Table 3 shows the results, which seem to indicate that Judy may have some appeal after all, given certain favorable circumstances. To help us perceive the effects more clearly, we summarize the results in Table 4.

TABLE 4   Mean Number and Percentage of Sign-ups "With Judy Paragraph" and "Without Judy Paragraph" Among Freshmen and Seniors*

Class	With Judy Paragraph		Without Judy Paragraph		Mean Total	
	Number	Percent	Number	Percent	Number	Percent
Freshmen	7.00	35	6.67	33	6.83	34
Seniors	17.33	87	4.00	20	10.66	53
Mean total	12.16	61	5.33	27	8.74	44

* Hypothetical data.

If we interpret the data in Table 4 as two simple experiments, we are led to the conclusion that both maturity and motive appeal had effects. Considering only the mean total *column*, we note that only 34 percent of the freshmen volunteered, whereas 53 percent of the seniors did. Considering only the mean total *row*, we note that with Judy as a motive appeal 61 percent of the students volunteered, whereas without her only 27 percent did.

Both of these statements, of course, are oversimplified interpretations. Maturity, by itself, did not have a positive effect on volunteers, because within Table 4 the seniors "without Judy" make up the lowest proportion. Further, the motive appeal, by itself, did not have a positive effect, because among the freshmen, the "Judy paragraph" makes no appreciable difference. The effect is an *interaction*—enhancement of one variable by the other.

To make this relationship more clear, we construct Figure 6, where *FJ* stands for "freshmen with Judy paragraph," *FO* stands for "freshmen without Judy paragraph," *SJ* stands for

												SJ	SJ		SJ
SO SO SO															
	FJ FJ			FJ											
FO		FO	FO												
. .	. . .	. .	. .	.	.	.	.	.	.	.	.	.	.	.	.
15 20 25	30 35 40	45	50 55	60	65	70	75	80	85	90	95				

Figure 6 Distribution of Proportions for "Freshmen with Judy Paragraph" (**FJ**), "Freshmen without Judy Paragraph" (**FO**), "Seniors with Judy Paragraph" (**SJ**), and "Seniors without Judy Paragraph" (**SO**)

"seniors with Judy paragaph," and *SO* stands for "seniors without Judy paragraph."

We observe from Figure 6 the following results of our experiment:

1. As in the first experiment, the freshman classes overlap considerably in the "with Judy paragraph" and "without Judy paragraph" conditions.
2. The seniors in the "without Judy paragraph" condition apparently are even more reluctant to volunteer for experiments than the freshmen in either condition. The overlap between the seniors in this condition and the freshmen is relatively slight.
3. The seniors in the "with Judy paragraph" condition are clearly more willing to volunteer than any other group.

These results cannot be accounted for by the effect of either variable alone or by the effects of the two variables simply added together. Therefore, an interaction exists between maturity and motive appeal.

After celebrating our successful solution of the problem, we meet again to consider further the implications of the results. We now have a way of getting senior men to volunteer for our experiments, but we still have no way of recruiting freshman men. Again, the senior faculty member speaks:

The experiment we've just conducted indicates that our theoretical position was a proper one. Judy does facilitate volunteering, and the reason she doesn't work for the freshmen is an inhibition effect she carries with her. That is, our appeal puts the freshmen in an approach-avoidance conflict, and we know what effects such a conflict has.

We'd like to bring the level of freshmen who volunteer up to the level of our seniors. I suggest that the easiest way to do that would be to try some things that might lower the inhibition level of the freshmen.

I have two things in mind. First, I think that part of the inhibition comes from having girls from the class present when the appeal is made. I suggest that when we make the appeal we excuse girls from the class. Second, we've already talked about the probable reason for the freshman reluctance. The boys say to themselves, "If I sign up, I'm admitting I can't get a date on my own." I therefore suggest that we make a confederate of the most attractive boy in the class (Judy can be the judge), instruct him to volunteer first, and see if the others don't follow. I should think the others would then say to themselves, "If he's willing to admit he'd like a date with Judy, I'm willing too." In other words, we'll plant a little opinion leadership in the group.

Approving this advice, we decide to design a third experiment that will serve as a check on our previous results as well as a test of the new hypotheses. The design (see Figure 7) is a three-dimensional one, an $A \times B \times C$ design in which variable A is maturity (freshmen and seniors), variable B is motive appeal ("with Judy paragraph" and "without Judy paragraph"), and variable C is counterinhibition (with females, without females, and without females plus opinion leader). Each of the 12 blocks in Figure 7 represents 3 classes.

Our previous research, together with our rationale, permit predictions about the proportion of volunteers from each block relative to all other blocks. These predictions are expressed in the equation below, where F stands for "freshmen," S stands for "seniors," J stands for "with Judy paragraph," O stands for

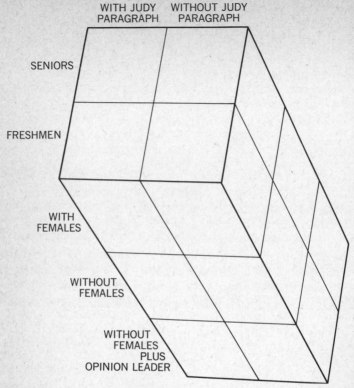

Figure 7 A X B X C Design

"without Judy paragraph," W stands for "with women present," X stands for "without women present," and L stands for "with opinion leader acting as confederate." The symbol $>$ means "will be greater than."

$$SJXL = SJX = SJW = FJXL > FJX > FOXL > FJW =$$
$$FOW = FOX = SOXL > SOX = SOW$$

Interpreting this concise set of predictions will be easier if we notice certain of its features. The equation is arranged in such a way that everything to the left is either equal to or greater than everything to the right. Term by term, our predictions are as follows: All the senior classes in which the "Judy" appeal is made will be about equal. In the first experiment using seniors we managed to recruit an average of 87 percent by using the "Judy" appeal. We cannot expect to improve on that high proportion by removing women from the sign-up session or by providing an opinion leader. The fourth term ($FJXL$) stands for "freshmen/with Judy paragraph/without women present with opinion leader." We expect the proportion in this condition to reach the high sign-up level achieved by the seniors in the earlier experiment. We expect this condition to be superior to all the other freshman conditions. The fifth term (FJX) represents "freshmen/with Judy paragraph/without women present." We expect the absence of women to remove some inhibition from the men. Therefore, this condition should be better than all the other freshman conditions except the one where women are absent and an opinion leader is active. The sixth term ($FOXL$) represents "freshmen/without Judy paragraph/without women present/with opinion leader." The fact that we make this condition superior to conditions the freshmen have undergone in previous experiments simply indicates that we expect the opinion leader to have some effect in his own right, regardless of Judy. The seventh, eighth, and ninth terms all represent freshman classes that we consider to be equivalent to those we manipulated in the first experiment. We have no reason to predict that any class will be better than the others or better than the freshmen participating in the first experiment. The tenth term ($SOXL$) stands for "seniors/without Judy paragraph/without women present with opinion leader." We expect the opinion leader to have some effect in his own right for the seniors as well as for the freshmen. Therefore, we predict that these classes will produce more volunteers than will the senior classes that have neither the "Judy paragraph" nor an opinion leader (the classes represented by the last two terms).

Table 5 shows the results of the study. Because the figures are hypothetical, we will pretend that the proportions in this study are identical to comparable proportions in the second

TABLE 5 Number and Percentage of Sign-ups in Twelve Experimental Conditions*

	Freshmen with Judy Paragraph		Freshmen without Judy Paragraph		Seniors with Judy Paragraph		Seniors without Judy Paragraph	
	Number	Percent	Number	Percent	Number	Percent	Number	Percent
Women Present								
Class A	10	50	7	35	16	80	4	20
Class B	5	25	9	45	19	95	3	15
Class C	6	30	4	20	17	85	5	25
Women Absent								
Class D	15	75	6	30	18	90	2	10
Class E	13	65	9	45	17	85	6	30
Class F	14	70	5	25	19	95	4	20
Women Absent, Active Opinion Leader								
Class G	20	100	12	60	18	90	3	15
Class H	18	90	15	75	19	95	4	20
Class I	16	80	16	80	20	100	5	25

* Hypothetical data.

experiment wherever blocks represent the same conditions. The array of numbers in Table 5 is more confusing than helpful. Therefore, we construct Table 6, which summarizes the data.

To make sure that we do not make the mistake of calling chance differences real, we construct Figure 8 to show relative amount of overlap among the various conditions, using the same notation scheme we employed for making our predictions. The symbol F stands for "freshman," S for "senior," J for "with Judy paragraph," O for "without Judy paragraph," W for "women present," X for "women absent," and L for "opinion leader active."

In our hypothesis, we had predicted first, that the optimum conditions would be $SJXL$, SJX, SJW, and $FJXL$. Examina-

TABLE 6 Mean Number and Percentage of Sign-ups in Twelve Experimental Conditions*

	Freshmen				Seniors			
	With Judy Paragraph		Without Judy Paragraph		With Judy Paragraph		Without Judy Paragraph	
	Number	Percent	Number	Percent	Number	Percent	Number	Percent
Women present	7.00	35	6.67	33	17.33	87	4.00	20
Women absent	14.00	70	6.67	33	18.00	90	4.00	20
Women absent, opinion leader active	10.00	90	14.33	72	19.00	95	4.00	20

* Hypothetical data.

tion of Table 6 and Figure 8 bear out this part of the hypothesis. The four conditions are far toward the high end of the proportion scale. They overlap considerably with each other but not much with the other eight conditions. Second, we predicted that the next best condition would be *FJX*. Again, the data confirm this part of the hypothesis. Our third prediction was that the next best condition would be *FOXL*. The data do not confirm this part of the hypothesis. The *FOXL* condition was equal, not inferior, to the *FJX* condition. Apparently, the opinion leader was as potent a force for these freshmen as the motive appeal, or else the absence of women from the motive appeal condition left a considerable amount of inhibition still operating. We also predicted that the next four conditions (*FJW*, *FOW*, *FOX*, *SOXL*) would be equivalent. Depending on how we interpret the data, this part of the hypothesis may or may not be confirmed. The *SOXL* does share much of the distribution of the other three conditions. However, it seems to be more closely clustered with the following conditions, *SOX*

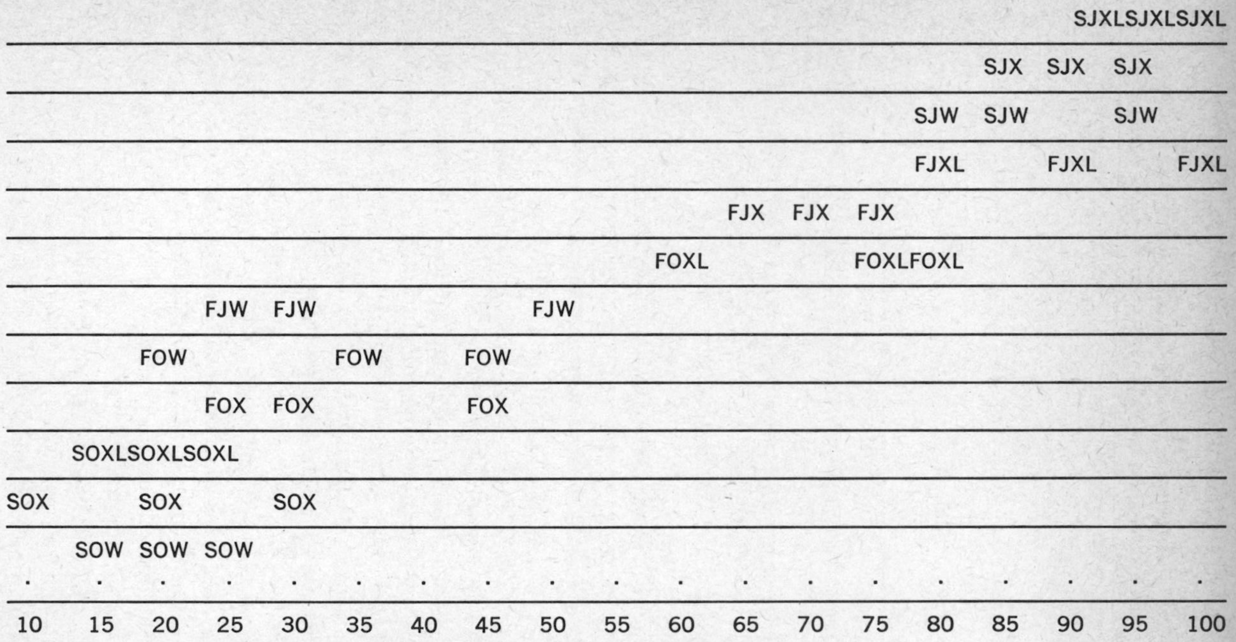

SJXLSJXLSJXL

SJX SJX SJX

SJW SJW   SJW

   FJXL   FJXL FJXL

FJX FJX FJX

FOXLFOXL

FOXL

FJW

FOW FOW FOW

FOX

FJW FJW

FOX FOX

SOXLSOXLSOXL

SOX SOX   SOX

SOW SOW SOW

SOX

10	15	20	25	30	35	40	45	50	55	60	65	70	75	80	85	90	95	100

Figure 8 Distribution of Proportions in Twelve Experimental Conditions

and *SOW*. Therefore, we interpret only the first three conditions as being equivalent, categorizing *SOXL* with the last two conditions. Apparently, for these seniors, the opinion leader by himself had very little effect. Lastly, we thought that *SOX* and *SOW* would be equivalent and least effective. This part of the hypothesis is confirmed, but we add *SOXL* to this most inferior category.

Complex designs are not limited to three dimensions, though we have difficulty picturing more than that. We can design experiments to test interactions among variables with as many dimensions as the problem seems to demand.

One important variation on experimental design permits us to control differences among subjects in the various experimental conditions. The designs that have been considered so far in this chapter have *between-subjects* variables—each experimental condition has in it a different set of subjects. The fact that each human being is unique adds considerably to the uncontrolled forces operating in the experiment. This uncontrolled variation can sometimes be eliminated by using the same subjects for different experimental conditions. The variables so treated are then *within-subjects* variables.[2]

A few years ago, Charles Houck and I attempted to discover some of the effects of regional dialects in persuasive speeches.[3] Our hypothesis was that in general Northerners would be more effectively persuaded by speakers using a Northern dialect than by speakers using a Southern dialect, and that this identification effect would be enhanced when the proposition of the speech was relevant to regional attitudes.

We devised two persuasive messages, each about 1,000 words long. One message, against integration of Southern colleges, was clearly relevant to regional attitudes. The other, against government aid to needy college students, was not so clearly relevant to region.

We chose our two speakers from a pool of four native Southerners, all of whom could produce at will either their native Southern dialects or their acquired Northern dialects. We eliminated one speaker from the pool because his delivery of the speeches in Southern dialect sounded almost evangelistic, indicating differences other than those in pronunciation. Another speaker's Southern dialect was of a variety that subjects in a pilot study did not perceive as clearly Southern, and we eliminated him from the study. The two speakers we chose produced dialects that were clearly perceived as Northern and dialects that were clearly perceived as Southern by subjects in the pilot study.

Each speaker recorded each speech in each dialect. The tapes were introduced to the college classes used in the experiment as "the first in a series of exercises in critical listening." One speaker was alleged to be "Larry Markham, Professor of Sociology, Tulane University"; the other was introduced as "Robert Howard, Professor of Anthropology, Wake Forest University."

The variables of this three-dimensional experimental design (represented in Figure 9) were: (1) topic (integration and gov-

Group	Topic	Dialect	Speaker
I (32 subjects)	Integration	Southern	Howard
	Government aid	Northern	Markham
II (32 subjects)	Government aid	Southern	Markham
	Integration	Northern	Howard
III (32 subjects)	Government aid	Southern	Howard
	Integration	Northern	Markham
IV (32 subjects)	Integration	Southern	Markham
	Government aid	Northern	Howard

Figure 9 A Three-Dimensional, Within-Subjects Experimental Design

ernment aid); (2) dialect (Northern and Southern); and (3) speaker (Howard and Markham). We arranged our experimental treatments in such a way that each group of subjects heard two speeches. In the combination of speeches, each group was exposed to each level of each of the three variables. Each subject in each group heard a speech on integration and one on government aid, a speech in a Northern dialect and one in a Southern, a speech by Howard and one by Markham.

The results partially confirmed the hypothesis. The speech irrelevant to regional norms was more effective in the Northern dialect than in the Southern dialect. For the other topic, however, the Southern dialect made the speaker seem more competent (though not more trustworthy) to Northern listeners than the Northern dialect did.

PROBLEMS OF MEASUREMENT

The concept of *operational definition* has already been discussed at some length, and has been applied to the variables in a few hypothetical experiments. This section will be concerned with operational definition (that is, measurement) of a few variables commonly employed in communication research.

Communication experiments generally attempt to specify either (1) the effects personal and environmental variables have on the *messages* produced by a *source* or (2) the effects *messages* have on *receivers*. The hypothetical experiment that was conducted early in this chapter, in which an attempt was made to discover the effects of presence of the mother on children's vocalizing behavior, was of the first type. The other three hypothetical studies, which attempted to discover the effects of variations in messages on recruiting volunteers for communication experiments, were of the second type.

The first type of study requires measurement of messages. Scholars often call the methods by which this measurement is accomplished *content analysis*.[4] Content analysis is a research method designed to insure reliable measurement of variables in the manifest content of a communication. In general, the method requires nine steps: (1) formulation of general hypotheses; (2) selection of sample of messages to be analyzed; (3) selection of categories, or classes of things to be quantified (for example, indicators of anger) and units, or kinds of things to be put in the classes (for example, words, clauses, or sentences); (4) formulation of judgmental procedures; (5) selection of control or normative data; (6) reformulation of general hypotheses in terms of categories and units; (7) selection of criterion for accepting or rejecting hypotheses; (8) tabulation; and (9) application of criterion. A study of the content of suicide notes in the next chapter illustrates this method.

One of the thorniest problems involved in content analysis is the fourth step mentioned above, formulation of judgmental procedures. Many persons are notorious for their unreliable understanding of messages. The content analyst should take at least the following precautions:

1. He should define his categories with words whose common meanings denote the variables he is interested in.
2. He should define his units carefully so that his coders will know, for example, whether they are to make judgments on words or sentences.
3. He should survey material similar to the material that he intends to analyze to discover the relative difficulty of the judgments to be made.
4. He should prepare a list of explicit instructions for his coders to use in assigning units to categories. This list of instructions should include illustrative material and possibly a lexicon specifying certain commonly occurring units for certain categories.
5. Using those instructions, coders should independently assign material similar to the material that will be coded in the main analysis.
6. He should check inter- and intracoder reliability.
7. He should revise his instructions.

The second type of study, in which the experimenter attempts to predict and confirm the effects of messages on receivers, most frequently involves one or more of three kinds of dependent variables: actual behavior, retention, and attitude.

We considered a case of using behavioral outcomes as a measure of effect in our series of experiments requesting volunteers for experiments. The effect we were interested in was signing up on a volunteer sheet. To measure that effect, we simply counted the number of volunteers. The kinds of behavior that might be measured are limited only by the experimenter's ingenuity. He might attempt to make sophisticated physiological measurements. Or he might attempt to measure intensity and duration of laughter. Or he might attempt to measure the force with which subjects push a button in response to a communication.

A whole methodological literature has grown up around attempts to measure the retention of messages. One method that is simpler than most and apparently as reliable as any is called *cloze procedure*. Using this method, the experimenter simply reproduces his messages with every fifth, or tenth, or fifteenth word deleted. He then gives these doctored messages to his subjects and asks them to fill in as precisely as they can the missing words. A subject's score is the number of words he fills in exactly right. A cloze procedure test of your retention of the preceding paragraph looks like this:

> We considered ——— case of using behavioral ——— as a measure of ——— in our series of ——— requesting volunteers for experiments. ——— effect we were interested ——— was signing up on ——— volunteer sheet. To measure ——— effect, we simply counted ——— number of volunteers. The ——— of behavior that might ——— measured are limited only ——— the experimenter's ingenuity. He ——— attempt to make so phisticated ——— measurements. Or he might ——— to measure intensity and ——— of laughter. Or he ——— attempt to measure the ——— with which subjects push ——— button in response to ——— communication.

Similarly, the measurement of attitude has been a perennial problem in the social sciences. Most experimenters in communication seem to have settled for a rather simple method devised by Charles Osgood and his associates: the *semantic differential* technique.[5]

The semantic differential technique involves the use of bipolar adjectival scales. For attitude, these scales involve the use of such evaluative adjectives as "good" and "bad." The adjectives have blanks between them, and the subject is required to place a check mark in the blank most nearly representing his attitude toward the concept being judged. Usually, the experimenter scores the test by assigning a value of 7 to the blank at the "good" end of the scale, a 1 to the blank at the "bad" end, a 4 to the "neutral" blank, and so on. Following is a single-scale semantic differential test of your attitude toward a concept:

Going to Class Today

	7	6	5	4	3	2	1	
good	— :	— :	— :	— :	— :	— :	—	bad

Frequently, research aimed at measuring the effects of communication has as one of its principal interests the subjects' perception of the source of the communication.[6] This perception repeatedly has been shown to be related to the persuasive effectiveness of a message. Two elements in this perception that seem to be especially important in enhancing a speaker's effect are most commonly called *trustworthiness* and *competence*, and several studies have been carried out to devise appropriate semantic differential scales for the measurement of these characteristics. Below is a semantic differential test of your perceptions of a communication source. The first four scales are for trustworthiness, the last four are for competence.

THE AUTHOR OF THIS BOOK

	7	6	5	4	3	2	1	
admirable	_ :	_ :	_ :	_ :	_ :	_ :	_	contemptible
honest	_ :	_ :	_ :	_ :	_ :	_ :	_	dishonest
just	_ :	_ :	_ :	_ :	_ :	_ :	_	unjust
kind	_ :	_ :	_ :	_ :	_ :	_ :	_	cruel
experienced	_ :	_ :	_ :	_ :	_ :	_ :	_	inexperienced
expert	_ :	_ :	_ :	_ :	_ :	_ :	_	ignorant
trained	_ :	_ :	_ :	_ :	_ :	_ :	_	untrained
competent	_ :	_ :	_ :	_ :	_ :	_ :	_	incompetent

SUMMARY

This chapter has focused on problems inherent in designing experiments ranging from the most basic to the most complex. An examination was made of the overlap in ranges of scores as well as the differences in averages in an attempt to discover ways of guarding against unjustified conclusions due to chance fluctuation. To overcome bias in experimental design, both random and stratified random selection of subjects were utilized. The section on more complex designs was concerned especially with discovering the effects of interaction among variables. Experiments designed in such a way that some variables operated within, rather than among, subjects were found to utilize subjects most efficiently. Finally, mention was made of some problems in the measurement of behavior, retention, and attitude that arise only in communication research.

Notes

1. John Stuart Mill, *A System of Logic* (8th ed.; New York: Longmans, 1930).

2. See E. F. Lindquist, *Design and Analysis of Experiments in Psychology and Education* (Boston: Houghton Mifflin, 1953).

3. Charles Houck and John Waite Bowers, "Dialect and Identification," *Language and Speech* (in press).

4. For a fuller treatment, see John Waite Bowers, "Content Analysis," in Phil Emmert and William D. Brooks (eds.), *Communication Research Methodologies* (Boston: Houghton Mifflin, in press).

5. Charles E. Osgood, George J. Suci, and Percy H. Tannenbaum, *The Measurement of Meaning* (Urbana: University of Illinois Press, 1957).

6. For example, see John Waite Bowers and William A. Phillips, "A Note on the Generality of Source-Credibility Scales," *Speech Monographs*, XXXIV (1967), 185–186.

3

Applications of
Experimental
Design
in
Communication
Research

The first two chapters of this book have treated abstract notions. Almost all of the studies discussed have been hypothetical ones, invented to illustrate the concepts of experimental design. This chapter will be concerned with real research applying those concepts.

The first part of the chapter will describe a series of studies carried out by a six-person seminar for research in group communication. These studies are previously unpublished, and an analysis will be made here of their methodological shortcomings. All the studies are attempts to discover new laws governing rumor transmission.

The second and third parts of the chapter will deal with illustrative studies of the two types defined late in Chapter Two: (1) a series of studies relating source variables to the messages they produce, and (2) studies relating message and source variables to their effects on receivers. The third section will discuss a study concerned with the effects of a message variable only and a series of studies concerned with the effects of an interaction between a message variable and a source variable.

An understanding of the studies reported (except for the statistical analysis) is not beyond the capabilities of those who have carefully read the first two chapters. In view of this fact, the analyses of the experiments will contain as little reference as possible to technical matters.

SOME RESEARCH ON RUMOR

In the fall semester of 1967–1968, five University of Iowa graduate students enrolled in a seminar that I conducted to do research in group communication. Among the six of us, three had previously carried out experimental studies in communication and three had not. We decided to analyze the phenomenon called rumor.[1]

Our review of the experimental literature revealed that previous studies of rumor had led to the following generalizations:

1. Rumors change in content, depending on the motivational structure and linguistic habits of the transmitter and his perception of these elements in his receivers. These changes may be loss of detail (leveling), elaboration of some elements (sharpening), or distortion (assimilation).

2. Rumors tend to be eliminated or correctively modified by persons in a state of "critical set." Such persons bring to bear frames of reference external to the rumor during reception, and these frames of reference affect later transmissions in the direction of greater plausibility.

3. Rumors are most likely to be spread when the consequences of the event with which they are concerned have strong relevance for the potential spreaders or when the antecedents and/or consequences of the event are

highly ambiguous. This last condition means specifically that official accounts and interpretations either are withheld or unavailable for other reasons, or that official sources are untrustworthy. Relevance and ambiguity together are sometimes referred to as "involvement."[2] Their importance to rumor is reinforced by a mass of research on information diffusion.[3]

As a group, the seminar carried out six studies of rumor that had in common the planting of a rumor or an event that might be expected to give rise to rumor, the opportunity for interaction among potential spreaders, and a later questionnaire requesting various kinds of information about rumor-spreading conversations and about speculation concerning the antecedents and consequences of the rumor. The following account of these studies will attempt to provide partial answers to the following empirical questions: (1) What characteristics of a message or event make it amenable to spreading? (2) What characteristics of the people involved make spreading likely? (3) Given appropriate messages, events, and potential participants, what is the nature and extent of the rumor network? (4) How do the tone and content of conversations change during the sequence of conversations? (5) Do women differ from men in their rumor-spreading characteristics?

As will become apparent, the first four studies have relevance only to the first question. The last two studies provide information that answers the first question as well as all the others. The first section of the report will include short descriptions of all six studies.

Characteristics of Message or Event

The messages planted in the first four studies all met the two criteria that previous studies had indicated were necessary antecedents to rumor—each message was relevant to potential spreaders and was ambiguous in some respects. Yet these messages did not give rise to rumors.

FIRST STUDY. Subjects in this study were 39 students, mostly juniors, taking the course "Analysis and Criticism of

Communication Arts." As was customary in the course, the students had earlier been organized in 6 small groups for a discussion during the 50-minute Friday class meeting. The chairman of each group was made a confederate and was instructed to plant a rumor in the group, attributing it to the instructor's research assistant. Two types of rumor were employed: a "good news" rumor that the class would be required to write one less paper in the course than had previously been announced, and a "bad news" rumor that the class would be required to write one additional paper.

In addition, previously gathered data made possible the manipulation of two other variables. A week earlier, the instructor had administered a questionnaire under the pretext of gathering information to form permanent discussion groups in the class. Data from these questionnaires were used in the rumor study to appoint three high-credibility and three low-credibility chairmen to initiate the rumor. Also, three of the groups formed were extremely cohesive in that the members had indicated on their questionnaires that they would like to continue working with each other. The other three groups were not cohesive. In summary, the experimental design was three-dimensional, the variables being: (1) nature of rumor; (2) credibility of source; and (3) group cohesiveness.

The study was inconclusive. Both rumors failed to spread in spite of their relevance and ambiguity.

SECOND STUDY. The first study led us to suspect that relevance and ambiguity might be inadequate as a description of the essential antecedents of rumor. However, interviews with some of the subjects in that study indicated that they wrote so many papers in their courses that one more or one less may not have been important enough to be relevant. Therefore, we invented new rumors for the second, third, and fourth studies, which we carried out almost simultaneously.

In the second study, we used students in one section of a course on Radio Production. Again, the class was divided into small groups. A rumor about the form and content of an upcoming midsemester examination had been planted earlier with two of the students. We thought that these subjects would begin to spread the rumors spontaneously and therefore did not make them confederates. They failed to spread the rumors, in spite of the message's relevance and ambiguity. Again, we had an inconclusive study.

THIRD STUDY. This study used as subjects the students in another section of the course on Radio Production. The class was divided into small groups. This time, the fictional rumor that was planted concerned the exceptionally low distribution of grades achieved on the midsemester examination, which was now over. Again, the rumor did not spread, in spite of its relevance and ambiguity.

FOURTH STUDY. The fourth study was more complex than the second and third. Two sections of the freshman speech and composition course, both taught by the same instructor, were subjects. These students were told to meet in small groups to discuss an assigned reading. On the day before the discussion, the instructor had met in his office with one student from each of the small groups. He mentioned to these students in passing that, as a result of recent political demonstrations on campus, the Iowa Legislature might institute strict class attendance regulations at the university. The following day, a note was planted in each small group, ostensibly from the instructor, stating that strict attendance would be required in his class beginning immediately after Christmas vacation. (This instructor had not previously enforced any attendance requirement.) We anticipated that the students who had been in his office on the previous day would relate the note to the message they had received from him, giving rise to speculation among all the students in the group.

These classes had filled out the same sociometric questionnaire used in the first experiment. On the basis of the questionnaire data, we controlled amount of cohesiveness in the groups. We also segregated the groups by sex. Thus, we had a two-dimensional design, the variables being cohesiveness and sex.

The fourth study, like the others, was inconclusive. The notes planted in the discussion groups prompted almost no conversation within the groups.

CRITICISM OF THE FIRST FOUR STUDIES. Our main problem in the first four studies was that we failed to learn the right things from our mistakes. We had assimilated the analytic system dictating that if a verbal message had relevance and ambiguity for potential spreaders it would spread. For that reason, we assumed that the message we planted in each succeeding study lacked either relevance or ambiguity. The thought should have occurred to us earlier that relevance and ambiguity in a message are not necessarily sufficient cause for rumor. In fact, one of the earlier experiments we had surveyed was unsuccessful in producing rumor in spite of what seemed to be a relevant and ambiguous message.

Although not nearly so severe, a second shortcoming of the research was a lack of sufficient control over some aspects of the rumor situations. Each instigator of rumor probably should have been made a confederate of the experimenters. Under those circumstances, at least a first transmission of the message would have been assured. Also, a number of subjects in one study (the fourth) did not appear for class the day the rumor was planted. We should have provided stronger motivation for class attendance that day, thereby assuring that the situation as it occurred would correspond more fully with the situation as we had planned it.

Our experience with the first four studies led us to speculate that relevance and ambiguity by themselves were not sufficient conditions to give rise to rumors. In the fifth and sixth studies, we attempted to remedy our problems by staging dramatic events involving unresolved conflicts. The antecedents and consequences of these events would have some relevance and ambiguity for our experimental subjects.

FIFTH STUDY. Subjects in this study were members of three freshman speech and composition classes, all in the honors program and all taught by the same instructor. One student from each class was employed as a confederate. In the 7:30 A.M. and 8:30 A.M. classes, the procedure was as follows:

> During a regularly scheduled class period, the instructor was conducting a series of impromptu speeches. Ten minutes after

the beginning of the period, a man dressed in a suit, tie, and overcoat entered the classroom and asked the instructor to step out in the hall with him. The instructor said that he was busy teaching class, but the man replied that what he wanted was important and could not wait. The instructor and the man then left the room and engaged in conversation in the hall. Within a few minutes, while the instructor was still absent, the confederate entered the room, apparently arriving at class late, and said to the students who were within hearing range: "What's going on out there? I heard this guy in the suit say to [instructor's name], 'We've decided to give this class to another instructor.' Then [instructor's name] said, 'What the hell do you mean? There's got to be another way to handle it.' Does anybody know what's happening?" A few minutes later the instructor re-entered the classroom, gathered his books and motorcycle helmet, handed what was apparently a corrected theme to the confederate, who had entered late, and left without a word. Another instructor then entered, announced that he was taking over the class for the regular instructor, and proceeded with the impromptu speeches. He offered no explanation, and replied "I don't know" to any questions about the instructor, the event, its antecedents, and its probable consequences. In addition, at the conclusion of the period he instructed the students to come to class the following day.

The procedure was precisely the same in the 11:30 A.M. class, except that the confederate, on entering the room late, took his seat without saying anything.

The following day, in the three classes combined, the subjects reported a total of 134 conversations on their questionnaires (an average of 3.27 per student). We had no way of measuring how far accounts of and speculation about the event went beyond this first-level transmission. Apparently, the event itself, without the account of the hallway conversation by the confederate, was enough to give rise to rumors. Members of the 11:30 A.M. class, in which the confederate said nothing, reported an average of 3.19 conversations per person, almost as many as the all-class average.

Criticism of fifth study. We were much more fully satisfied with the fifth study than we had been with the first four. One element was not well controlled: The confederate in one class spoke loudly enough upon entering the room that all students in the class heard him. In the other class, a few students were out of earshot. We should have devised a way to keep this stimulus constant in the two classes where confederates spoke. Further, we wished later that we had found a way to check our inferences about the rumor network beyond the first level of transmission by witnesses.

SIXTH STUDY. Subjects in this study were students in the course, "Introduction to Graduate Study in Speech and Dramatic Art." Just before the end of a Wednesday meeting of the class, the following event was staged, involving one of the three instructors in the course and a student, both of whom were acting as confederates. The syntax sometimes seems strange because this is a direct transcript from a tape recording.

STUDENT   I've got a question. Now I assume we are going to have another one of these papers we're going to write. And I can't see where anything you've said has been very helpful in telling me, somebody who's not a director or someone like yourself, who knows all about the theater, how it's going to be very helpful in doing one of these assignments. Can you give a specific example . . .

INSTRUCTOR   Well, I don't think I would worry if I were you, Mr. ————. I don't think I would worry so much about whether my lectures are helpful or Professor ————'s or on historical criticism or whatever. It seems to me, though, that it might be helpful to you, for instance, to get in the papers, the assignments. And if I recall correctly, Professor ———— did not find among his souvenirs your fourth assignment.

STUDENT   Oh. That's that historical bit.

INSTRUCTOR   That's right. And I'd like to know when you are going to get it in. Because we've all . . .

STUDENT   Well, I haven't done it yet. And I don't know how you do the goddam thing. Unless I feel I get some contribution here that, you know, helps me to know how to do . . .

INSTRUCTOR What?

STUDENT I just may not do the goddam thing. Just like I may not do this goddam thing unless I find out, you know, something that's a little more helpful to me in doing these kinds of assignments.

INSTRUCTOR Well, I'm, I'm . . . I don't know about Mr. —————, but I'm certainly sorry if that's the way you feel about it. But I do think that if that is the way you feel about it, then you probably ought to leave the class now. And I don't think you ought to come back . . .

STUDENT You're kidding!

INSTRUCTOR Until you are willing to make some kind of apology to Professor —————, —————, and, I suppose, even me. So why don't you leave?

STUDENT You mean you're kicking me out of class?

INSTRUCTOR Yep.

STUDENT (rising to leave) This is the first time I've been kicked out of a class since seventh grade.

INSTRUCTOR I would say that it's more of the nature that you are kicking yourself out. Peace.

The following Friday, a rumor was planted in the class detailing the consequences for the student, given certain contingencies. This rumor did not spread. However, the event itself gave rise to substantial rumor behavior independently of the planted message. The questionnaire administered at the Monday meeting of the class, five days after the event, revealed that the 30 students had participated in 77 conversations concerning the event.

Criticism of sixth study. Again, we erred in failing to control adequately the origin of our planted rumor. Our confederate told it to one person who, in turn, told it to his wife and no one else. Another weakness of the sixth study was the lapse of two days between the event and the planted rumor and the lapse of five days between the event and the questionnaire. As we learned later when we analyzed the data from the study, most of the conversations about the event occurred within 48 hours. Rumors had run their course by the time we planted a rumor. The further lapse of three days meant that many conversations probably were forgotten before subjects had a chance to report them. Finally, the sixth study, like the fifth, had no mechanism for examining conversations that were carried on between nonwitnesses at levels beyond the witness level.

Conclusion about Characteristics of the Message or Event. The six studies taken together seem to indicate that previous answers to the question of which characteristics of a message or event make it amenable to rumor have been inadequate. In addition to relevance and ambiguity, some dramatic element seems to be required. Our experience shows that unresolved conflict is one such element that, together with relevance and ambiguity, constitutes sufficient reason for rumor. This dramatic element may be even more important than relevance and ambiguity. The incident in the sixth study had no particular implications (relevance) for the future lives of the rumor spreaders, yet accounts of it traveled far and fast. In the fifth study, opportunity existed to eliminate ambiguity by communication either with the instructor or with the administration of the freshman speech and composition program. Yet only 3 of the 41 students involved attempted to confirm or deny through official sources their speculations about the incident's implications. Perhaps most people take some joy in ambiguity.

Characteristics of People Involved

From the subjects in the fifth and sixth studies, we selected for follow-up interviews 8 *centers,* subjects who had participated in the maximum number of conversations (4) that could be reported on in the questionnaire. We then matched these 8 with 8 *controls* drawn from the remaining subjects. All selections were random, except that we deliberately drew the same number from the freshman classes as from the graduate class, and we deliberately distributed the sexes evenly over the center and control conditions. Two subjects were unavailable, so the resulting pool of interviews consisted of 7 centers and 7 controls. Of these, 1 center and 1 control were freshman nen, 2 centers and 3 controls were freshman women, 2 centers and 2 controls were graduate men, and 2 centers and one control were graduate women.

The interview was designed to reveal the subjects' habitual communication behavior. It requested certain personal data, then asked the subjects to recount the environment and content of their conversational activity from the time they arose on the morning of the interview until 5 hours later. Most interviews were tape-recorded. All were analyzed with a standard 28-item form, most by someone other than the interviewer. The analysts, for the most part, did not know whether any given interview was of a center or a control.

Because of the small number of subjects involved in this part of the study, the results should be viewed with some skepticism. However, many of them confirmed our expectations and a few were suggestive of future research.

Among the freshmen involved in this part of the study, the most interesting difference between centers and controls was the reference groups with which they identified. The 3 centers identified strongly with their peer group—roommates and classmates. None of the 4 freshman controls had peers as their strongest reference group. Two identified themselves with a relatively well-defined group of older students in fine arts, one identified with her family, and one revealed no particular reference group in the interview. For the graduate students, on the other hand, reference groups did not distinguish successfully between centers and controls. From their interviews, we inferred that almost all identified most strongly with fellow graduate students in the department. The 2 groups taken together seemed to indicate that individuals are unlikely to be centers in rumor transmission unless they have a reference group identification with people to whom the event has relevance but that not all who identify with those people become centers. This conclusion led to speculation that some of the controls might have been centers, had the event been particularly relevant to their reference groups.

However, the interviews did result in identifiable differences between centers and controls other than differences in reference groups. Table 7 shows those differences that seemed to be most reliable.

TABLE 7 Means for Centers and Controls on Various Interview Items

Item	Mean for Centers	Mean for Controls
Trips home per semester	1.85	3.29
Number of conversations reported	6.71	7.42
Length of reported conversations (minutes)	11.85	6.86
Tendency to seek or avoid conversation	2.57*	3.57*
Number of reported conversations initiated by interviewee	4.71	2.99
Number of reported conversations directed by interviewee	3.57	1.14
Number of incidental conversations reported (chance meetings)	2.71	5.29
Number of reported conversations about specific persons	1.29	.85
Number of people involved in conversations identified by name in interview	4.28	2.00
Number of stereotyped conversations reported (how are you, when are your finals, etc.)	2.50	4.29

* This judgment was made by the analysts on a seven-level scale. The smaller number indicates stronger conversation-seeking behavior.

The first line in the table, "trips home per semester," probably reflects only the reference group difference. Controls identified with their families more strongly than centers did, especially among the freshmen. The other items indicate that centers in our study were more likely to seek, initiate, and direct conversations in their everyday behavior than were controls. The conversations of controls were more likely to be incidental—to occur in passing. Furthermore, the conversations of centers were more likely to be about people and less likely to be stereotyped than were conversations of controls. Finally,

he centers were more likely to identify by name (and to know
by name) those with whom they conversed. These last two
findings might indicate that centers for this kind of rumor
transmission are more people-oriented and that controls are
more thing- and event-oriented, both in the content and the
tone of their conversations.

Extent and Nature of Rumor Network

The 41 freshmen involved participated in 134 reported conversations. These conversations involved 105 reported nonwitnesses, and we had no way of knowing how many independent
conversations the nonwitnesses had with other nonwitnesses.
In the graduate class, 30 subjects responded to the questionnaire
and reported participation in 77 conversations involving 44
nonwitnesses. Again, we had no way of knowing how many
independent conversations the nonwitnesses had with other
nonwitnesses. Because the questionnaire in this class was administered 5 days after the event, we suspected that a number
of conversations had been forgotten and were not reported.

Most of the nonwitnesses contacted by both groups were
university students. However, considerable numbers of wives,
other relatives, and sweethearts became involved, and one
freshman girl even called her parents long distance to report
the incident and speculate about its implications. One graduate
student reported talking about the event in three separate conversations—to her husband, a neighbor, and the director of a
play in which she was appearing. The relevance of the event
to any of these individuals probably would be minimal, but
this subject turned out to be one of the communication centers
in the study. She was an extremely fluent subject, and she
may have found that her liveliness enabled her to persuade her
listeners of the event's interest value to them.

Among the freshmen, 15 participants reported conversations
that involved members of more than one class. The effects of
this part of the network will be discussed in the next section.

Geographically, the scenes at which conversations occurred
shifted during the sequence of conversations. Among the fresh-

men, the first conversation was more likely to occur at the scene of the event than at any other place. The second was more likely to occur in another class or in a cafeteria than at any other place. The third was most likely to occur in the subject's dormitory room, and the fourth was more likely to occur in another class the next day or in the subject's room than at any other place. The kinds of relationships among graduate students with regard to geography and sequence were much the same, except that transmissions were more likely to occur in the subjects' homes or other students' homes than among the freshmen. In general, as the sequence of conversations grew, the perimeter of the locations expanded.

Temporally, the tendency to talk about an event decelerated rapidly. The freshmen had only 24 hours between the event and the questionnaire. Of the 134 conversations reported, 85 occurred in the first 3 hours of the 24. The graduate students had 5 days between the event and the questionnaire. Of the 77 conversations they reported, 41 occurred during the first 3 hours of this period; only 10 conversations were reported later than 48 hours after the event.

Beyond statements about temporal deceleration and geographic broadening, generalizations about the network were difficult to make from our data. Given a situation of unresolved conflict whose consequences have some relevance and ambiguity for witnesses, conversations about the event reached more nonwitnesses than there were witnesses. Presumably, the nonwitnesses initiated conversations with other nonwitnesses, especially those to whom the event might have been expected to have direct or indirect (for example, wives) relevance, but our data said nothing about the extent of this second-level network.

Changes in Tone and Content

We classified the tone of conversations into three types: "giving information," "receiving information," and "interactional." For most subjects, the first two conversations were with other witnesses to the event, and as might be expected, they were primarily interactional (75.9 percent of the 79 conversations among the freshmen were interactional, 20.2 percent gave information, and 3.7 percent received information). In the third and fourth conversations, the interactional tone maintained its majority (63.6 percent of the 55 conversations), but giving information became more common (34.5 percent). Receiving information was reduced in the third and fourth conversations to 1.8 percent.

These findings are not surprising. The first and second conversations were almost all among witnesses who engaged in mutual evaluation and speculation (interactional). Later conversations often involved nonwitnesses, and speakers had to give information if the event was to be a topic of conversation at all. Many conversations with nonwitnesses then became interactional, but some did not.

Changes in the content of the conversations were intriguing. Three types of statements could be distinguished: factual (statements about the event itself), evaluative (expressions of speakers' attitudes toward the event, the people, and the institutions involved), and speculative (inferences about the antecedents and consequences of the event). The first and third types of statement could be analyzed for their validity, their correspondence to fact. Statements of the second type, evaluation, could not be so analyzed, but they could be analyzed for intersubjective agreement.

For the freshmen, the factual accounts of the event that were given on the questionnaire differed very little. Most accounts indicated that the instructor's manner implied more anger than he thought he had implied. Phrases like "then he stomped out of the room" were common. One interesting difference shows the role of relevance in retention. All accounts for the 7:30 and 8:30 A.M. classes reported that the confederate entered late and delivered his account of the dialogue in the hall. In the 11:30 A.M. class, where the confederate entered late but said nothing, only one student produced a statement on the questionnaire about the confederate's late entrance.

We classified the freshmen's speculative statements about antecedents of the event in five categories: (1) the instructor had done something to cause him to be fired; (2) the instructor had some problem (sickness in the family, and so on) at home; (3) the instructor was in trouble; (4) the situation had been contrived with the consent of the instructor; (5) no conclusion was possible. The first three of these could be interpreted as inaccurate, the fourth as accurate, and the fifth as indecisive. Table 8 shows changes among the frequencies in the five categories over time.

As can be seen, a majority of the early speculations about the event (61 percent) were inaccurate. The rumor process reduced this inaccuracy to only 28 percent of the reported conversations on the ensuing day. Apparently, at least in this case, rumor changed speculation in the direction of greater accuracy. The largest percentage of later conversations (43 percent) reached no conclusion. Most of these conversations expressed two conflicting conclusions—either that the instructor had been fired or that the situation had been contrived. Reporting subjects expressed a wait-and-see tendency in these conversations, apparently feeling no strong discomfort from the uncertainty. The percentage of conversations reaching accurate speculation rose to 30 percent in later conversations.

The process of correction occurred through three mechanisms. First, of the 134 reported conversations, 15 involved members of more than one of the instructor's classes. When two students from two classes reported to each other essentially the same event, the strong possibility of a contrived situation immediately became salient. Most of these conversations, as well as others involving the same corresponding accounts at two or three levels beyond the original conversations, reached the conclusion that the situation had been contrived. However, some students reached no conclusion even on this basis, and one girl continued in her belief that the instructor had been fired.

Second, a few conversations were with nonwitnesses who had previously taken a course under the instructor or who knew him personally. These nonwitnesses served a strong corrective function by suggesting the possibility that, given the instructor's personality and interests, the situation had been

TABLE 8 Frequency and Percentage* of Various Speculations about Antecedents of the Event over Time

					Inaccurate						Total
	Fired		Problem at Home		In Trouble		Contrived Situation		No Conclusion		
Time of Conversation	Number	Percent	Number	Percent	Number	Percent	Number	Percent	Number	Percent	
During the event, remaining portion of class, and immediately after class	15	34	2	4	10	23	9	20	8	18	44
Within following 23 hours	22	24	0	0	2	2	27	30	39	43	90

* Percentages do not equal 100 because of rounding.

contrived. Subjects who had previously thought that the instructor had been fired moved to the indecisive or accurate conclusion categories on the basis of these conversations.

Third, a few subjects brought to bear their knowledge of the instructor and critically adopted more accurate explanations without the aid of others. Upon reflection, these subjects recalled earlier experiences with the instructor leading to the inference that he was capable of contriving such a situation. Later conversations involving these subjects were also likely to move those with whom these subjects interacted from one of the inaccurate categories to the indecisive category. In general, correction proceeded by application of information that was either not available or not salient at times close to the event itself. We concluded that in general, rumors served a corrective function when such information was available in the network. Also, temporal distance from the event changed some subjects' uncritical set to a critical one.

Most of the speculation among the freshmen was about the antecedents of the event. Only a few freshmen reported conversations about consequences. The conclusion that the instructor had been fired, of course, clearly led to the inference that a new teacher would be forthcoming. A small number of students reported that they had talked about persuasive strategies to adopt toward the new instructor. One vowed to give him or her as much trouble as possible. However, in later conversations most students reached either the accurate or indecisive categories. Because neither of these types of conclusion would result in any appreciable consequences, the number of statements expressing consequential speculation was negligible.

Of the 41 freshmen, 28 expressed some evaluation of the event at the time it occurred, when many of them thought the instructor had been fired. The greatest number of these, 12, were unhappy about it and thus expressed a positive evaluation of the instructor and a negative one of the firing agent or agency. The second greatest number, 11, expressed mixed emotions; most of them indicated that they approved of the action but disapproved of the manner in which it was carried out. Four students were unequivocally happy about the firing asumption and thus expressed a negative evaluation of the instructor and a positive one of the firing agency. One student imply expressed anger at the firing agency for the manner in which it had conducted the event. All of these evaluations, of course, depended upon faulty speculation about the actual ntecedents of the event. Such evaluations did not seem to have ffected appreciably the readiness with which subjects received corrective information when it was available to them, although one of the students who disliked the instructor persisted in holding and communicating her belief that he had been fired, even after she learned from a member of another class that he same event had happened there. Clearly, a wish-fulfilling kind of selective perception was at work in her.

In the graduate class, nearly all the reported conversations included only factual and evaluative statements. Speculation about antecedents and consequences was practically nil. We attributed this difference between graduates and freshmen to a difference in the events rather than in the nature of the samples. The freshman event permitted many more hypotheses among the witnesses, for it was less complete. The graduate incident, on the other hand, could be considered an almost complete action, including causes and some effects; it was much more fully witnessed than the freshman event. Furthermore, the conclusion of the freshman event (firing) had clearly relevant consequences for the subjects. Unobserved consequences of the graduate event, on the other hand, probably would have clear relevance only for the one student directly involved. At any rate, the reports of the graduate students included only one speculation by one subject: that the student in he incident would apologize.

Most conversations in the graduate class included more than one evaluative statement. The most frequent kind was a negative evaluation of the student's choice of words (52 instances). Next came positive evaluations of the sentiments expressed by he student (18 instances). Other evaluations expressed were 7 negative statements about the professor's role in the event and 7 expressions of approval for his handling of it. No subject expressed approval, at least in questionnaire responses, of the language used by the student. A few evaluations went far beyond the incident itself. Students expressed attitudes toward the department (6), toward the university (4), and toward the world in general (3). We did not record the direction of these few evaluations.

The graduate data gave us some opportunity to analyze for factual distortions. Each respondent wrote an account of the original incident, and we could check these accounts against our tape recording. The resulting clues to selective perception and retention were interesting, though our analysis was on a simple level.

The following statements, taken directly from subjects' accounts of the incident, may give some evidence of motivational systems' effects:

[The student] referred to [the instructor's] lecture as Mickey Mouse. (Subject 01)

[The student said] "None of this stuff is useful." (Subject 05)

[The instructor made] the comment that [the student] did not appear to be trying. (Subject 06)

[The student] tended in tone to imply that he thought it all a lot of hogwash. (Subject 07)

Finally [the student] concluded with something to the effect that the entire course lacked content and direction on assignments. (Subject 10)

[The student] implied that this [lack of relevance of lectures to assignments] was especially the case with [this instructor's] lectures. (Subject 17)

[The instructor] became irritated, took the defensive, and . . . (Subject 21)

[The student] questioned the value of an instructor imparting knowledge pertaining to an assignment after the assignment was due rather than before. He then refused to hand in the assignment in question and swore, generally, at [the instructor] (Subject 23)

[The student said] "It seems that this class is designed to help us learn the art of successful thesis writing and we haven't covered enough information to allow me to write my third assignment." (Subject 26)

[The instructor said] "And I don't think you should return

until you offer apology to Professor ————, the class, and
even me." (Subject 25)

In general, rumor serves a corrective function when relevant
information is available in the network. Rumor almost always
includes factual information and evaluation, but it prompts
speculation about antecedents and consequences only if the
event as seen was an incomplete action and/or if unknown
consequences have relevance to the subjects. Distortion
through selective perception and retention occurs in the life of
a rumor. One subject maintained her wish-fulfilling belief about
the consequences of the event even in the face of overwhelm-
ing contrary evidence.

Men and Women

The graduate sample differed from the undergraduate sample
in comparative rumor behavior of men and women. Among the
graduates (6 women and 24 men), we could find no differences
at all. Among the freshmen, on the other hand, we found substantial differences.

Of the 41 freshman witnesses, 24 were males and 17 were
females. The men engaged in 71 conversations, whereas the
women were involved in 63, so that on the average, males had
2.98 conversations and females had 3.70, or nearly one more
conversation per subject.

Freshman men differed from freshman women also in the
tone of their conversations and in the conclusions reached by
the conversations. Of the female conversations, 33 percent
were of the information-giving variety, whereas only 20 percent of the male conversations were in this category. Both sexes
had the same proportion of receiving-information conversations
(3 percent), and the males had more interactive conversations
(77 percent compared with 64 percent for females). In conclusions reached during the conversations, women were most
likely to decide that the instructor had been fired (43 percent);
only 14 percent of the conversations involving male subjects
reached that conclusion. The most common category for

male conclusions was the indecisive one. Table 9 summarizes these differences between freshman males and freshman females.

TABLE 9   Differences in Rumor Behavior of Freshman

Criterion	Males	Females
Average number of conversations engaged in	2.98	3.70
Percentage of conversations giving information	20	33
Percentage of conversations receiving information	3	3
Percentage of interactive conversations	77	63
Percentage of conversations reaching inaccurate conclusions (instructor fired, problem at home, instructor in trouble)	25	52
Percentage of conversations reaching accurate conclusion (contrived situation)	30	24
Percentage of conversations reaching indecisive conclusion	45	24

Of the students we interviewed about habitual communication behavior, 6 were men and 8 were women. Table 10 shows the categories in which this sample of men and women differed substantially from each other.

The data in Table 10 are compatible with our other data and also with some of our cultural stereotypes. Women, in general, participate in more and longer conversations than do men. Men initiate a greater proportion of their conversations than women do, as we would expect, because our culture encourages initiative by males and receptiveness by females. This tendency is also shown in the comparative conversation-seeking ratings of the two sexes. Finally, women are more likely to be gossipy (indulging in idle chatter about people) than are men.

All the data taken together require some interpretation. Two findings are especially intriguing: (1) intersexual differences found among freshmen were not found among graduate students; (2) conversations of freshman women, though the

TABLE 10 Differences Among Fourteen Men and Women Interviewees

Criterion	Mean for Men	Mean for Women
Communications (phone calls and letters) home per month	1.66	4.00*
Gossipiness	6.17†	4.71†
Number of conversations	6.33	7.71
Number of people involved in all conversations	6.17	12.09
Length of average conversation (minutes)	5.66	10.50
Rating of conversation-seeking behavior	2.33†	3.54†
Number of conversations initiated by interviewee	5.17	2.71
Number of incidental conversations	3.00	4.73
Number of conversations about people	.83	1.21
Number of conversations about things (tests, etc.)	5.33	4.00

* This mean was raised by the behavior of one freshman girl who communicated with her home 15 times a month.

† These were ratings by analysts on a seven-point scale. The lower number indicates more of the behavior. Thus women were rated as more gossipy than men, but men were rated more conversation-seeking than women.

average number was higher, reached a greater proportion of inaccurate conclusions than did conversations of freshman men.

A number of studies have indicated rather general differences in the verbal behavior of men and women in our culture. Men, for example, are more physically aggressive than women when frustrated, but women are more verbally agressive, both in amount and quality, under frustrating conditions.[4] The culture seems to encourage this kind of difference in sex roles. Little boys should act; little girls should talk. The strong, silent role is a permissible, even desirable one for men but not for women. In most groups where the sexes are mixed, women carry the conversational burden. For men in our culture, talk is usually instrumental in reaching goals; for women, talk may be a goal in itself. Therefore, our discovery that freshman women talked more often about the incident than did freshman men is not surprising.

What is surprising is that the same differences did not hold for the graduate students. Assuming that the differences found for the freshmen were typical of our culture, the graduate sample was not typical. The graduate men may have been atypical, or the graduate women may have been atypical, or both groups may have been atypical. A number of hypotheses might account for the absence of differences. Taken together, these interpretations seem to account for most of the difference.

1. The small sample of graduate women (six) might well have been unrepresentative of graduate women in general.
2. The selection process by which most women (or men) become graduate students might be of such a nature that not many of those who fit the cultural stereotype survive it.
3. The process of formal education might change the communication differences between men and women so that differences between the sexes among college seniors, for example, would be somewhere between the large differences found for the freshmen and the absence of differences found for the graduate students.
4. The graduate women might have perceived the incident as less relevant to the people with whom they normally conversed than the graduate men did. Insofar as their networks differed from the male networks, they might not have perceived the incident as salient to the same degree that men did.

No bases can be found upon which to make choices among these alternatives. Some common sense evidence seems to exist for all of them.

The finding that freshman women reached a much higher proportion of inaccurate conclusions about the antecedents of the event than freshman men did is also somewhat perplexing. If, as the data seem to support, rumors about this event had a corrective effect, then freshman women, having participated in more conversations, should have reached more accurate conclusions. Yet the data indicate that they did not.

One way of reconciling the data and the speculation might be to consider the conversations in series rather than as a group. If rumor had a corrective effect for freshman women as it did for the sample as a whole, then most of the inaccurate conclusions should have occurred in the early conversations of the women. Analysis bears out this explanation partially but by no means totally. Table 11 presents relevant data for freshman men and women,

TABLE 11   Percentage of First, Second, Third, and Fourth Conversations Reaching Three Types of Conclusions, by Sex*

Conversation	Inaccurate		Accurate		Indecisive	
	Men	Women	Men	Women	Men	Women
First	44	58	7	21	48	21
Second	19	50	24	28	57	22
Third	29	47	50	24	21	29
Fourth	8	43	62	29	31	29

* Not all percentages equal 100 because of rounding.

Women were initially less accurate in their conclusions than men; moreover, the difference between the two groups became greater, rather than smaller, by the fourth conversation. The process of correction operated minimally for the women; its operation for the men was dramatically more effective. Women jumped to more inaccurate conclusions faster and held them longer.

Barring a significant difference in the habitual critical set of the two sexes as they were represented in the sample, the only logical explanation for these differences is that the networks employed by the men transmitted more corrective information than those employed by the women, insofar as the networks were different. This explanation is tenable if several relevant characteristics of the instructor and the subjects are considered.

1. The instructor was connected with a university-sponsored project that was located in one of the men's dormitories so that male students who lived together could attend class together. One of the classes in the experiment, the 7:30 A.M. class, contained male students from this "live-and-learn" project. These male students probably knew the instructor better than most of his other students did, and their communications extended beyond their own number to other students, primarily male.

2. Some of the corrective conversations involving members of more than one class occurred in natural science laboratories. To the extent that male students are more likely than female students to be participating in such laboratories, correction was more likely for the males.

3. Of the 41 subjects, 24 were male and 17 were female. To the extent that freshmen are more likely to converse with members of their own sex than with members of the opposite sex, this numerical advantage for males increased the possibility that corrective conversations involving members of more than one class would occur.

4. The two sexes may have habitually perceived the instructor differently (the males with suspicion, the females with acceptance), either because of his behavior or because of a sex role identification. Of course, suspicion would be more likely to lead to accurate conclusions than would acceptance, giving the males an advantage.

Summary

These six studies of rumor indicate that conditions beyond relevance and ambiguity are sometimes necessary for the spread of rumor. Unresolved conflict is one kind of event that fulfills this requirement. Indeed, subjects in one study seemed to take some satisfaction in the ambiguity of the situation, and subjects in the other study observed a situation only tangentially relevant to them. Given unresolved conflict, together with some relevance and ambiguity, rumors spread far and rapidly.

Rumors, in general, run their course rapidly. After a day, the events used in our studies seldom gave rise to conversations. Rumors are likely to be spread most by those who strongly identify with the reference group to which the rumors are relevant. These people also are likely to be generally more loquacious than is the norm for their group, are likely to be more seeking and directive in their communication behavior, and are likely to talk more about people and to know more people by name.

Changes in tone resulting from different kinds of auditors and changes in content resulting from selective perception and retention occurred in our studies. Rumors had a tendency to correct erroneous early speculations about the antecedents of one of the events. This procedure is likely to occur when relevant information is available in the rumor network.

Freshman men and women differed substantially in their rumor behavior, but these differences did not hold for graduate students. Among the freshmen, women talked more often than men, reached more inaccurate conclusions than men, and held to those conclusions more tenaciously than men. We attributed these differences to the relatively stronger presence of corrective information in the male network, as well as to cultural differences between the sexes.

Criticisms

Methodological. Probably the greatest methodological weakness in the series of studies was the failure to control independent variables adequately. In the two successful studies, we manipulated events and attempted to discover the effects of those manipulations. We had no control condition with which to compare the experimental conditions. Therefore, the two studies were more descriptive than experimental. We predicted the results in only the most general terms. (For example, we predicted that the events would give rise to rumors.) Hence the probable absence of any generalization in our discussion (except, possibly, the one requiring a dramatic incident as an antecedent to rumor) that approaches the status of a scientific law.

We also had problems in measurement. Our objective was to find out, as fully as possible, what course the rumors followed and what happened to them in the process. Our questionnaire, subject as it was to the frailties of human recall, was not the most direct method of getting this information. Ideally, we would have had tape recordings for analysis of all conversations (those among nonwitnesses as well as those involving witnesses) containing rumor material. That, of course, was impractical. However, we should have been able to obtain tape recordings of a few conversations. If we had, we could have checked them against the questionnaire reports, thus establishing the extent to which we could have confidence in those reports. In fact, we did attempt to make a few such recordings, but the tapes were unintelligible.

The representativeness (or lack of it) of our sample was a problem. Like all scientists, we wanted to be able to generalize from our studies to as broad a population as possible. Practical considerations led us to use as subjects in our two successful studies freshman honors students and beginning graduate students in speech and dramatic art. Both of these samples are atypical of at least a few criteria, not only within American culture in general but even within the college culture. This lack of typicality made generalization even more dangerous than it is in the usual social science experiment. From one point of view, however, this atypicality might have made our studies more rigorous than most rumor studies have been. Honors or graduate status might be assumed to carry with it a stronger critical set than would be found in most segments of the population. If so, the processes of distortion that affected our sample should be even more common in the general population.

For some analyses, our sample was clearly not sufficient to permit confident generalization. Our interview analysis of communication centers and controls had only seven subjects in each condition. Data from these interviews thus yielded only hints, not laws. The entire graduate class contained only six women. Our analysis of sex differences in that class, then, must be considered very weak.

Finally, the time pressure of the academic semester prevented full utilization of information gained from one study in the design of the next. Almost always, we were simultaneously designing one study, analyzing another, and executing still a third. Therefore, our mistakes were likely to be repeated.

SUBSTANTIVE. Substantive matters are difficult to separate from methodological ones because the two kinds of problems obviously interact with each other. However, some statements can be made about our series of studies that are more sub-stantive than methodological.

First, we probably disproved the old relevance-plus-ambi-guity formula more than it needed to be disproved. A fuller analysis of earlier rumor studies, together with a more penetrat-ing look at our own results in our first studies, would have given us more efficiency in the series.

Second, the research was relatively unfocused and the con-clusions diffuse. Partly because of time pressure, none of the research was carried through to its natural conclusion (the establishment of scientific laws). The only really rigorous finding was that relevance and ambiguity, by themselves, do not necessarily give rise to rumor.

Finally, our research on rumor was not as theory-oriented as it might have been, in that it did not establish, alter, or refute any very general statements about human behavior or even communication behavior. We related only a few of our con-clusions to more general phenomena, notably those relevant to the male/female stereotype in our culture and those relevant to selective perception and retention. However, we expressed the relationship between our research and these more general statements as afterthoughts. The research itself was not de-signed to test such phenomena.

ENCODING SUICIDE NOTES

The second series of studies that will be considered here relates variables in sources to variables in the messages they produce. This particular set of studies is concerned with the effects of motivational variables on messages, a topic in communication that has been barely skimmed by research.[5]

We are all aware that we can detect, through communication, something about the internal states of others and that they can detect the same sorts of things in us. Probably, we are especially good at detecting the moods of those who are close to us, those with whom we spend a great deal of time. Probably, we learn this skill by a form of hypothesis-testing. We say to a close friend, "You're awfully edgy today, aren't you? What's the matter?" If he answers with certain kinds of statements, we think that we have confirmed our hypotheses about the relationship between his behavior and his internal state. We may even go farther to verify our hypotheses. We may say to mutual friends, "What was the matter with Jeanne yesterday?" Certain kinds of answers to such questions reinforce our guesses about the implications of behavior.

As pointed out in earlier chapters, such informal hypothesis-testing has inherent in it two problems. First, we tend not to operationalize our definitions of the variables. Suppose that, in the hypothetical situation where we notice a friend's tenseness, a stranger is present. If he asks us later how we recognized our friend's tension, we probably will have trouble replying. We will be inclined to say, "I just know him so well, I could tell." Such a statement, of course, is not very helpful from a scientific point of view.

Second, we tend to be unable to generalize from one situation or one individual to another. Constant observation of one friend might lead us to conclude that he shows tension by social withdrawal—he broods. We might note about another that her tension is made manifest in a continual stream of trivial chatter. A third, more versatile friend might betray anxieties by brooding when with her family, chattering when with casual acquaintances. We might make these individual observations somewhat useful to science by calling them case studies, but our generalizing ability would be severely limited.

If we analyze the variables involved, we might note that they fall into two classes: (1) a content class, the things talked about; and (2) a stylistic class, the way they are talked about. If a close friend says, "My wife told me last night that she intends to leave me," we might infer from the content that the friend is experiencing some anxiety, depending on our prior perceptions about the nature of his relationship with his wife. If he says, "It's a nice day today," but avoids eye contact and speaks in a very low voice, we might infer from the style that he is experiencing anxiety. As we will see, both classes of variables are useful in communication research as scientific indicators of extreme motivational states.

The study made by Charles Osgood and Evelyn Walker was an attempt to relate research and theory in motivation to research and theory in language. In a way, Osgood and Walker chose a difficult set of materials when they decided to analyze suicide notes as indexes of motivation. In the first place, suicide notes are written, not spoken; Osgood and Walker thus lost all the visual and aural phenomena many of us use as cues to motivation. In the second place, suicides obviously are not available for further research. Therefore, many of Osgood and Walker's theoretical premises necessarily were unverified assumptions. This criticism will be discussed more fully after a discussion of the study itself.

Osgood and Walker took as the basis for their predictions a commonly accepted set of statements about motivation, both animal and human. According to these statements, which are backed by appropriate research, each of us has learned habits, and we respond to appropriate stimuli with these habits. However, some of our habits may be appropriate to the same stimuli but incompatible with each other. If I am hungry, for example, and I have 15 cents in my pocket, I may be faced with the choice of buying a doughnut or buying a piece of cake, but I cannot buy both. Which of the two I buy depends on the strength of the motivation and on the environmental cues. According to the theory, these competing habits are somehow arranged in hierarchies of alternatives—that is, one is more probable than another. Furthermore, the strength of the drive interacts with the strength of the habit in such a way that as the drive becomes stronger, the dominant responses in the hierarchy become more probable. "This means that behavior under increased drive, including [language] behavior, should become more *stereotyped*—the alternatives selected at all choice points should tend to be the most familiar, the most often practiced, the most expected." [6] This increase in predictability occurs only up to a point, however. Under extreme drive conditions, competing habits interfere with each other, producing disrupted behavior. In general, then, strong drives produce dominant behavior; extreme drives produce disrupted behavior.

Not all habits are associated with the same drives, of course. Nobody does deep knee bends to allay hunger. Some alternatives are appropriate to one drive, some to another. When two motives are operating simultaneously, these habits should conflict. Osgood and Walker were also looking for evidence of this kind of conflict.

The Sample

Osgood and Walker made what superficially seems to be a sound assumption: People writing suicide notes are in a high drive state. If they are, then the structure and content of their notes should contain elements reflecting this high drive state. To establish these elements, of course, Osgood and Walker needed other written materials to use as control conditions. They proceeded in two steps.

In the first step, they gathered two sets of materials. They secured a sample of 100 genuine suicide notes, 50 by men and 50 by women. They needed a control sample produced under similar conditions except that the drive state of the writers was to be lower. The suicide notes were, almost without exception, written to close friends and relatives; Osgood and Walker thus reasoned that ordinary personal notes among close friends and relatives might be an adequate control at this early stage of the research. They collected a set of such notes from a panel of men and women being used for other research purposes in a metropolitan area. However, they encountered another problem: Many of the suicide notes were very short, whereas the criteria to be applied required messages of at least 100 words. To solve this problem, Osgood and Walker decided to discard, for the purposes of most analyses, all messages of less than 100 words. This deletion left them with a sample of 40 suicide notes by males, 29 suicide notes by females, 13 control notes by males, and 59 control notes by females. Because the encoding differences between the sexes were minor and not germane to their hypotheses, we will ignore them and consider that the first step was to assemble 69 suicide notes and 72 control notes. Osgood and Walker applied to these notes a large set of stylistic and content criteria, which will be discussed later.

They picked what seemed to be the most promising of the criteria used in the first step as tests in a much more difficult comparison that was made in the second step. Their sample in this step was composed of 33 previously unused suicide notes and a control group of 33 simulated suicide notes (pseudocide notes) written by individuals who were matched with the genuine suicides on the bases of age and sex. The second step, obviously, was the more crucial test of their hypotheses—that extreme anxiety can be detected by stylistic and content analysis. Even this step, however, leaves unanswered some important questions, as will be seen when the study is criticized later in this chapter.

Hypotheses and Results

FIRST-STEP HYPOTHESES. In the comparison of suicide notes with ordinary personal notes, Osgood and Walker tested in an exploratory way four hypotheses that logically followed from the theoretical position. Because they were searching for information as much as they were testing hypotheses (the real test would come in the second step), Osgood and Walker employed a number of criterion measures for each hypothesis.

Their first hypothesis, following from the notion that strong motivation results in choices that are high in the hierarchy of alternatives, was: "The greater the motivation level under which language encoding occurs, the greater will be the stereotopy of choices." [7] They tested this hypothesis with six criterion measures.

1. Average number of syllables per word. The evidence is strong that English speakers use short words much more frequently than long words. Therefore, short words should be higher in the hierarchy of lexical alternatives than long words. If they are, persons experiencing strong motivation (suicides) should use a greater proportion of short words.

2. Type/token ratio. This is a measure of vocabulary diversity obtained by dividing the number of *different* words in a passage by the *total* number of words, repetitions and all, in the same passage. People experiencing high drive should use fewer different words, proportionally, and their type/token ratio should be lower.

3. Repetition of phrases. This measure is, of course, related to the type/token ratio. Persons in high drive should be more repetitious (being able to make fewer choices) in structure as well as vocabulary.

4. Noun-verb/adjective-adverb ratio. Nouns and verbs are necessary to the construction of sentences in English. Adjectives and adverbs are not. Therefore, a proportionally high number of adjectives and adverbs is a measure of the degree to which the basic elements in encoding are qualified. Suicides should have a higher proportion of nouns and verbs because they should be less capable of subtle qualification. Their scores on this measure should be higher.

5. Cloze measure. This technique, which is one way of measuring predictability in messages, was discussed in the

preceding chapter. Cloze scores for the suicides should be higher.

6. Allness terms. Some evidence indicates that we find it easiest to think (and talk and write) in polarized, dichotomous, good-bad terms. If so, these kinds of terms—"always, never, forever, no one, everyone, and so on" [8]— should be higher in our hierarchies of alternatives. Osgood and Walker anticipated that these terms would occur proportionately more frequently in the suicide notes.

Osgood and Walker's second hypothesis was designed to account for those suicide notes encoded under such high motivation that disruption occurred. Only two criteria were used to test this hypothesis: structural disturbances ("misspellings, punctuation errors, grammatical errors, syntactical errors, and even clearly awkward constructions" [9]) and average length of independent segments. The latter obviously is a measure of the complexity in sentence construction. Osgood and Walker thought that the disruptive effects of extreme drive would preclude any appreciable amount of subordinating elements in the independent clauses of suicides.

The first two hypotheses were directed at the general effects of heightened drive. The third used a collection of measures designed to detect the content and style effects of the specific drive for self-destruction. Osgood and Walker used five criteria to test this hypothesis.

1. The distress/relief quotient. This is "a ratio of distress-expressing phrases to the sum of these plus relief-expressing phrases." [10] It should be higher for suicides.

2. Number of evaluative common-meaning terms. These are value-expressing terms like good, bad, notorious, reprehensible, angelic. Suicides can be expected to use more of them.

3. Positive assertions about self. These statements associate the writer with positive things and dissociate him from negative things. Suicides probably will use proportionately more of them.

4. Time orientation. Osgood and Walker thought that suicides would be oriented away from the present, toward either past or future.

5. Mands. These are verbal responses that specify their own reinforcement. That is, a mand "expresses a need of the speaker and . . . requires some reaction (immediate or delayed) from another person for its satisfaction." [11] Most questions, commands, and requests are mands. Osgood and Walker thought that suicides would use proportionately more of them.

Osgood and Walker's fourth hypothesis sought evidence of motivational conflict in the suicides. Three criterion measures were employed:

1. Qualification of verb phrases. People experiencing motivational conflicts should find it difficult to make unambiguous, direct assertions. In Osgood and Walker's example, the suicide might say "I tried to love you" or "I had to love you" instead of "I loved you." [12]

2. Ambivalence constructions. These are stylistic and content indicators that show rather directly conflict in the mind of the writer. Some of the words Osgood and Walker counted in this category were: but, if, would, should, because, well, however, maybe, probably, possibly, seems, appears, guess, surely, really, and except. Apparently, any assertion that indicated a "yes-and-no" answer to a hypothetical question was counted in this criterion. Suicides can be expected to use more of these words than nonsuicides.

3. Percent ambivalent evaluative assertions. These are sets of assertions divided in such a way that the same thing is referred to both positively and negatively. Osgood and Walker's example: "I love you, honey . . . You never trusted me . . . I always quarreled with you . . . I stuck by our marriage, though." [13]

FIRST-STEP RESULTS. In general, the results of their comparisons between suicide notes and ordinary personal letters strongly confirmed Osgood and Walker's hypotheses. For the first hypothesis (that suicide notes would exhibit greater stereotopy of choices), they found that the most reliable differences were for the type/token ratio, the repetition of phrases measure, the noun-verb/adjective-adverb ratio, and allness terms. Two of the measures, though showing results in the expected direction, were not statistically reliable—that is, the distributions in the two samples (average number of syllables per word and the cloze measure) overlapped considerably. The latter distribution showed results in the expected direction, and the difference between suicide and control notes was statistically significant for male but not for the female writers.

The second hypothesis was that some suicide writers would be laboring under such extreme motivation that encoding disruptions would occur. However, neither of their two measures, structural disturbances and average length of independent segments, showed the anticipated differences. In fact, one measure, length of independent segments, had a statistically significant (.05 level) difference in the opposite direction.

The third hypothesis, designed to detect content and style differences specific to the self-destruction motive, had five criteria. Four of these criteria showed significant differences in the expected direction: (1) the distress/relief quotient, (2) number of evaluative common-meaning terms, (3) positive assertions about self, and (4) mands. Mands were one of the most reliable discriminators between suicides and controls in the study. Only one measure in this category, time orientation, failed to show differences between suicides and controls.

The fourth hypothesis predicted that the suicide notes would show more content and stylistic evidence of motivational conflict than would the control notes. Osgood and Walker's analysis showed statistically significant differences in the expected direction for all three of their criterion measures in this category: qualification of verb phrases, ambivalence constructions, and percent ambivalent evaluation assertions.

The authors of the research must have experienced some satisfaction from the results of their first step. Of their 16 criterion measures, 11 showed statistically significant results in the direction predicted by their theory. Two more showed differences in the expected direction but with too much overlap to be considered reliable. Given the information from the first step, Osgood and Walker were now prepared to put their measures of motivational differences in encoding to the much more severe test of the second step, the comparison of a new batch of suicide notes with a control set of pseudocide notes—simulated suicide notes written by individuals who were matched with the real suicides on the bases of age and sex.

SECOND-STEP HYPOTHESES. Before they began to test their second-step hypotheses, Osgood and Walker decided to test their own intuition about the suicide style by independently taking each of the 33 pairs and attempting to identify each member of each pair as suicide or pseudocide. The authors showed amazing insight into the style. Walker identified correctly 31 of the 33 pairs, Osgood 26 of the 33. Such accuracy set them to wondering, of course, whether all the counting their quantitative measures required was worthwhile. Were ordinary human beings much more sensitive than the criterion measures to the effects of motivation on encoding? They decided to have 8 graduate students perform the sorting task. The students were much less successful, scoring, on the average, exactly half right, which is precisely what would be expected if they had sorted by a chance system (say, coin-flipping). Osgood and Walker apparently had trained themselves with their use of the criterion measures to identify the notes correctly.

For the second step, Osgood and Walker discarded the criterion measures that had failed to discriminate in the first step: structural disturbances, average length of independent segments, and time orientation. They eliminated measurements that were specific to the self-destruction topic: distress/relief quotient, number of evaluative common-meaning terms, and positive assertions about self. Finally, they discarded the cloze measure, because too few of the notes were long enough to make it sensitive to differences.

This left them with 9 measures to be applied to the notes: average number of syllables per word, type/token ratio, repetition of phrases, noun-verb/adjective-adverb ratio, allness terms, mands, qualification of verb phrases, ambivalence constructions, and percent ambivalent evaluative assertions. Again, the length problem was a thorny one. Because many of the notes were very short, Osgood and Walker used only 13 pairs in the second step. They applied all their measures to each pair of notes and identified as a suicide the member so indicated by 5 or more of the 9 measures. Finally, they enlarged the sample to 24 suicide and 18 pseudocide notes by disregarding pairing and using all notes of 100 words or more. To these samples, they applied each of the 16 measures used in the first step.

SECOND-STEP RESULTS. The first test in the second step, identification by a majority of the measures for the 13 pairs of notes, resulted in correct identification in 10 of the 13 cases. This result is considerably better than chance.

The second test gave a fresh look at the reliability of the 16 measures under the more rigorous conditions provided by the pseudocide notes. As Osgood and Walker had anticipated, the measures specific to the self-destruction motive (distress/relief quotient, number of evaluative common-meaning terms, and positive evaluative assertions about self) did not discriminate successfully. The two most successful discriminators in the comparison were the noun-verb/adjective-adverb ratio, a measure of stereotopy, and number of mands, a criterion for the self-destruction motive. In addition, one of the measures that had been unsuccessful in the first step, length of independent segments (a measure of disruption under extreme drive), reached statistical significance in the more rigorous second step. Finally, the number of ambivalence constructions was a reliable indicator in the second step but *in the wrong direction*. From all the analyses together, we probably would conclude that our best bets for identifying suicide notes in a comparison with pseudocide notes would be the noun-verb/adjective-adverb ratio, the number of mands, the proportion of ambivalent assertions, and the length of independent segments.

Finally, in addition to their formal tests of hypotheses, Osgood and Walker explored the suicide and pseudocide notes on a *post hoc* basis, just to see what they could find. Some of the results were interesting, especially a penchant for concreteness in the real suicide notes as opposed to philosophical abstractions in the simulated ones. Further, the suicide notes contained more terms of endearment and references to mother, as well as more simple-action verbs (as opposed to mental state verbs for pseudocides). These lexical analyses, although they were not included as criteria in the original hypotheses, lend some additional support to Osgood and Walker's first hypothesis.

In summary, the Osgood and Walker study lends fairly clear support to the proposition that motivation systematically affects encoding behavior. The comparisons give some support to all four hypotheses and strong support to three. Qualifying statements about that support will be made in the criticisms of this study later in the chapter.

Another Study

Independently of Osgood and Walker, Daniel M. Ogilvie, Philip J. Stone, and Edwin S. Shneidman also studied the characteristics of suicide notes.[14] (Shneidman was with the Suicide Prevention Center, and it was he who had supplied Osgood and Walker with their pairs of notes.) Ogilvie, *et al.* also matched their pairs of notes with pseudocide notes, but they devised their own control sample, matching the suicides on sex (all were male), race (all were Caucasian), religion (all were Protestant), nation of birth (all were born in the United States), age, and occupational level.

Ogilvie, *et al.* did not proceed from theoretical premises as Osgood and Walker did. They were simply concerned with finding practical ways of distinguishing suicides from pseudocides. In their explorations, they used a computer system called the General Inquirer for content analysis. This system matches words in a text with words in a dictionary, automatically assigning them to the categories specified by the dictionary.

The Ogilvie, *et al.* study gives strong support to the findings of Osgood and Walker. The overriding difference between suicides and pseudocides was the extreme specificity and concreteness of the references in the genuine notes. As a test of their success, Ogilvie, *et al.* attempted to discriminate among the pairs of notes using three criteria combined in a rather simple way:

1. References to concrete things, persons, and places (higher for genuine notes).
2. Use of the word "love" in the text (higher for genuine notes).
3. Total number of references to processes of thought and decision [similar to Osgood and Walker's "mental state verbs"] (higher for simulated notes).[15]

This combined measure discriminated correctly 30 of the 33 pairs.

Criticism

At first glance, the Osgood and Walker assumption that suicides, when they write their notes, are operating in a state of high motivation seems reasonable. Nevertheless, these notes are not ideal vehicles by which to study the effects of motivation on encoding behavior.

If this study is to be used as a measure of the effects of high motivation on encoding style, we should have rather strong assurance that the experimental subjects were, in fact, in a state of high motivation. If we had subjects who were alive, we could verify their high motivation by one of two methods: administer as experimental treatments manipulations that rarely fail to produce high drive, or question subjects after the experiment in an attempt to get at their introspective assessment of their own drive level. The use of suicides as experimental subjects makes any such measures impossible.

If we are thoroughly convinced that suicides are in a condition of strong motivation, of course, further assurances are unnecessary. But are we so convinced? Our own introspection and some research seem to indicate that we experience our strongest drive *before* making a decision, not *after* making it. When a suicide encodes his final note, has he already made the decision to kill himself? The answer is that we simply do not know. If he has already decided, his drive may be somewhat lower than earlier, though he still faces the uncertainties of the act itself and whatever follows it. At any rate, we can plausibly imagine that all or some suicides, at the time they write their notes, are in states of relatively weak motivation.

On the other hand, we need to consider the control group in the second step, the pseudocide group. If we pretend we are members of that group, we hear ourselves given the following instructions: "Imagine that you are about to commit suicide. You are to write your suicide note, your final message. Make your note sound as real as possible. Write as if you were actually planning to take your own life."

If we are like most people, any assignment of writing that we expect to be read by others increases our anxiety level, our motivation level, somewhat. But we begin the task. What should we write about? Disappointments, of course—justifications for our act. These recollections of frustrations bring them back almost in their full force, further strengthening our motivation. We say to ourselves: "Is suicide such an implausible act? Would it be impossible for me to do?" We are faced with a decision, strengthening our motivation even more. By the time we have written a few words, we are no longer pretending to be strongly motivated; our real feelings make pretense unnecessary.

Osgood admits the possibility, though he does not emphasize it, that the use of suicides as an experimental group has its problems. He writes about the results of the first step of the study:

> One expectation from theory definitely does not hold up; suicide notes do not display more disorganization of encoding skills, either in structural disturbances or in shortening of sentence segments. This could mean that the drive level of the suicidal writer is not extremely high, that these measures were inadequate, that our samples were not well matched, or that the theory is wrong.[16]

A few pages later, he describes the second step:

> Whether [the pseudocide writers] were able to imitate the style of suicidal people by generating the heightened emotional state

and then encoding accordingly, or simply by adopting a style of encoding available in their repertoire (through extensive reading, listening to plays, or the like) cannot be answered from our data.[17]

These criticisms, of course, do not lessen the validity of Osgood and Walker's results. Osgood and Walker, together with Ogilvie, *et al.*, did discover real differences between genuine and simulated suicide notes. The reasoning that attributes these differences to differences in motivational level, however, may be faulty. The pseudocides may have been as strongly motivated as the suicides. We have made a plausible case that they were. Because of the nature of the sample they selected, Osgood and Walker have no way of refuting our criticism. To do so, they would have to repeat the experiment using motives other than the self-destruction one and exerting more control over the manipulation and measurement of the motives.

A STUDY OF METAPHOR

An important, even dominant, set of questions in rhetorical and literary theory concerns the operation and efficacy of metaphors. In 1965 Michael Osborn (whose earlier work had been critical and historical rather than experimental) and I began what turned out to be a successful study to begin answering these questions in a scientific way.[18]

Osborn's credentials as a critic were flawless. His doctoral dissertation, executed under the direction of a leading rhetorical critic, Douglas Ehninger, and the linguistic philosopher Charles Morris, had analyzed the operation of metaphor in a number of famous speeches from the past. Osborn and Ehninger had published in 1962 an analytic article concerning the operation of metaphor that was partly based on this dissertation.[19] Osborn was following up that work with an intensive, multileveled analysis of various metaphors in a series of eighteenth-century British speeches.

My bias was as strongly scientific as Osborn's was historical-critical. My doctoral work had been under the direction of an important communication scientist, Samuel L. Becker, and had resulted in an experiment to examine the effects of a variable I called language intensity.[20] I had followed up the doctoral study with other scientific studies of the attitudinal effects attributable to variations in other aspects of linguistic and paralinguistic style.[21]

The story of our collaboration is, in itself, an interesting case study in communication. It began with conflict. At a small social gathering, Osborn and I found ourselves seated adjacently at the same table. Because of the similarity of our interests, the conversation inevitably turned, after phatic beginnings, to research on the operation of metaphor. Early in the conversation Osborn expressed the thesis that metaphor, aside from its artistic merits, is usually an effective rhetorical tool. In most instances, he said, a speaker using metaphor would have a greater effect on audiences than would the same speaker delivering literal counterparts of the same arguments. I dissented, maintaining that metaphor usually not only failed to help a speaker achieve his goals with an audience but often actually impeded him. I also tried to explain away Osborn's proposition by arguing that the aesthetic effects of metaphor deceived critics into failing to recognize its instrumental impotence.

As the argument progressed, both of us began to distort our own early statements, changing them into more polarized ones. What had "usually" been the case became, for both of us, "always" the case. Refusing offers of mediation from others at the table, we proceeded to make the dispute into a nose-to-nose confrontation. For Osborn, metaphor became rhetorically good, without qualification. For me, it became rhetorically bad, without qualification.

Osborn managed to produce two kinds of evidence for his thesis. First, he thought of the practice of apparently effective speakers from the past. When he formally encoded his arguments later, he wrote:

> Notable examples are Demosthenes' [an ancient Greek orator] "On the Crown" and Cicero's [an ancient Roman orator] "First Oration against Catiline," both of which develop in their con-

clusions the metaphors of sickness and pestilence; William Pitt's [an eighteenth-century British orator] "On the Abolition of the Slave Trade," which concludes with an elaborate light-dark metaphor; Lincoln's "First Inaugural Address," which ends in an interesting musical image; [William Jennings] Bryan's "The Cross of Gold," for which the closing imagery has come to provide the title; and Franklin Roosevelt's "First Inaugural Address," in which war imagery develops throughout the speech and culminates in the conclusion.[22]

All this sounded like strong historical evidence for Osborn's contention that metaphor is rhetorically effective.

In addition, Osborn appealed to the statements of rhetoricians—perceptive people who, without benefit of experimentation, made generalizations about the effects of variations in messages. Osborn summarized his argument:

> Principally, rhetoricians respect metaphor because it pleases the audience by enlivening the discourse in which it occurs, by appealing directly to the senses, by stimulating mental processes in a manner which is intrinsically pleasurable. Thus, Quintilian concluded shrewdly, metaphor "contributes to the case," since, in the process of pleasing, metaphor makes it easier to attend, disposes us to be grateful to the speaker who has provided this pleasure, and makes us receptive to his point of view.
>
> This gratitude to the speaker is one of the principal supports in traditional rhetorics for a second evident assumption, that metaphor enhances the credibility or *ethos* of a speaker. The traditional theorists never draw an explicit relationship between metaphor and ethical proof, but their analyses give ample basis for the supposition that such relationships do exist. In addition to Quintilian's notion of gratitude felt toward the speaker, both Cicero and Aristotle argue that apt and appropriate metaphor is taken by an audience as a sign of high mental ability.[23]

Osborn concluded from tradition that "we might expect the use of metaphor to increase audience respect for the speaker," and thus to enhance his effectiveness.[24]

My evidence against Osborn's thesis, though slight, was scientific, and I was able to keep the controversy from becoming a complete rout by referring to some of my own research. My

earlier studies of language intensity had shown that highly in
tense, emotional language, given certain kinds of situations
topics, and audiences, has *weaker* effects than more moderate
unemotional styles. Furthermore, my research had shown tha
metaphors, especially certain kinds of metaphors, are perceivec
as highly intense. The two kinds of metaphor I had found t
be most intense were those figuratively using sex ("all term:
generally associated with the practice of and traffic in the se>
act and related events" [25]) and death ("all terms whose usua
associations are with death, decomposition of the body, anc
the afterlife" [26]). Using these studies as evidence, I formulatec
the following argument:

> Under certain conditions, extremely intense language weaken:
> the attitudinal effects of persuasive messages.
> Sex and death metaphors are species of extremely intense lan-
> guage.
> Therefore, under certain conditions, sex and death metaphor:
> weaken the attitudinal effects of persuasive messages.

Osborn continued to disagree. The generalizations I had inferred from earlier scientific work were unacceptable to him.
On the other hand, Osborn's historical and critical generalizations were obviously unacceptable to me. Ultimately, we decided to collaborate on an experiment designed to test directly
the persuasive effects of metaphor. We wanted the experiment
to be a direct and fair test of the rhetorical power of metaphor.
Therefore, we wanted to place our metaphors in contexts that
were compatible to them. On the other hand, we wanted to test
only the power of metaphor; we did not want to confound the
metaphor variable with other message and situational variables.
Therefore, we discarded the idea of building an entire speech
around a metaphoric theme, for such a speech would put to
work more variables than simply the metaphoric one.

Reviewing my earlier experimental studies, we found that
the messages I had employed departed in two significant respects from what Osborn thought was the best rhetorical practice of the past. First, in the earlier studies, I had indiscrim-
inately mixed metaphorically intense expressions and literally

intense expressions. Possibly, Osborn thought, the two types of intensity differed in their effects, but their mixing in the earlier messages hid the rhetorical superiority of the metaphors. Second, we noticed that most of the speeches from the past that Osborn had cited reached their most intense metaphors in their conclusions. My earlier research had used metaphors throughout the experimental messages. Possibly, intense metaphors are effective only late in persuasive speeches, after the audience has been emotionally prepared for them.

Osborn, the rhetorician of the team, overcame these rhetorical weaknesses in the speeches he wrote for our experiment. We used two original speeches, each of which could conclude either with an intense, extended metaphor or with the metaphor's literal counterpart. (These speeches did not otherwise employ particularly intense language.) One speech was against protective tariffs and ended, in its figurative version, with an intense metaphor related to sex. The other speech, opposing government aid to needy college students, had in its figurative version an intense, death-related metaphor. The four conclusions were:

PROTECTIVE TARIFF, LITERAL. From what we've learned here today it is obvious that we have listened too long to the voices of those who represent special interest groups. Too long, we ourselves have stood by and permitted the ruination of our western economies by those who have proclaimed the doctrine of protective tariff. We have neglected our larger interests for the sake of the smaller interests of these special groups, and the result has been—not a vigorous, protected economy—but rather economic stagnation.

I say the time has come to listen no longer in our legislatures to these short-sighted lobbyists. For only when we shut our ears to them, and remove the tariff barriers which stand as so many harmful restrictions on our general welfare, can we achieve the goal of free trade, giving to the entire world new economic hope and a new sense of economic well-being.

PROTECTIVE TARIFF, METAPHORICAL. From what we've learned here today it is obvious that we have listened too long to the seductive whispers of special interest groups. Too long, we ourselves have stood by and permitted the rape of western economies by those who have proclaimed the doctrine of protective tariff. We have prostituted our own interests to satisfy the lust of these special interest groups, and the result of this impotent union has been—not a vigorous and healthy economy—but economic abortion.

I say the time has come to banish from our legislative chambers these economic seducers. For only when we shut our ears to them, and remove the barriers which stand like so many ill-advised parental restrictions, can liberty and economy lie side by side, stimulating each other, giving through free trade a new birth of hope to the world and a new manhood of economic well-being.

GOVERNMENT AID TO NEEDY STUDENTS, LITERAL. So today we must learn, I believe, that governmental aid is no substitute for individual initiative. Must we allow, then, our government to replace our own individuality? Can we afford to lose the basis of our national strength under the so-called protective influence of Washington? How soon will we learn that "freedom" and "individual" are interchangeable words? Will it be when, filled with the words of would-be idealists, we turn to find that freedom is no longer with us? I pray that we will not permit these things to happen, that we will come to realize that in education governmental help is not compatible with our national goals.

GOVERNMENT AID TO NEEDY STUDENTS, METAPHORICAL. So today we must learn, I believe, that governmental aid is no substitute for individual initiative. Must we allow, then, our government to slowly strangle our own individuality? Can we permit the basis of our national strength to rot away under the so-called protective influence of Washington? How soon will we learn that the death of the individual is the death of freedom? Will it be when, behind the sweet words of would-be idealists, we hear the sickening death rattle of liberty in the throat of America? I pray that we will not permit this gentle murder of our values, that we will come to realize that in education the kiss of governmental help is the kiss of death.[27]

Osborn and I were interested in the effects of the two kinds of conclusions, both on attitude change toward the concepts of the speeches and on judgments of the speakers. We used appropriate semantic differential scales to test both sets of hypotheses. The scales for judgment of the speakers were divided into three types: trustworthiness, competence, and ingenuity.[28]

Group	Speech	Conclusion
I (33 subjects)	Protective tariff	Sex metaphor
	Government aid to needy students	Literal
II (33 subjects)	Protective tariff	Literal
	Government aid to needy students	Death metaphor
III (33 subjects)	Government aid to needy students	Death metaphor
	Protective tariff	Literal
IV (33 subjects)	Government aid to needy students	Literal
	Protective tariff	Sex metaphor

Figure 10 Experimental Design for
Metaphor Study

The subjects in the study were college freshmen—the same kind of sample I had used in my earlier studies. Each subject heard both basic speeches, one with a metaphorical, the other with a literal conclusion. Although this procedure might have prompted the subject to form a mental preference for one speech or the other, we did not see this result as being due to a weakness in the design, for we wanted to discern any differences that existed, even if we had to force subjects to discriminate. Also, a design in which all subjects experience all conditions adds an important element of control to an experiment, for differences discovered in such a study cannot be attributed to initial differences among the subjects.

The results of the study were intriguing. Neither of the basic speeches effected more change in attitude toward its concept than did the other. However, both metaphorical versions of the speeches produced more change toward the concept than did their literal counterparts. These differences were substantial, and statistics indicated that they were unlikely to have been due to chance. In short, the experiment confirmed Osborn's hypothesis that intensely attitudinal metaphors, used in the conclusions of persuasive speeches, were more effective than literal conclusions.

Our second interest was in the effects of these metaphors on judgments of the speakers who used them. Here, we found an interaction between the two independent variables—metaphor and topic. On all three of the dimensions we measured—trustworthiness, competence, and ingenuity—the speaker on the protective tariff, who employed the sex metaphor, fared better than did the speaker on government aid to needy students, with his death metaphor. In fact, the speaker using the death metaphor received higher judgments on every dimension when he used his literal conclusion than when he used his metaphorical one, whereas the speaker using the sex metaphor always received higher judgments in the metaphorical condition than in the literal one.

A number of explanations could account for these different effects of the two basic speeches. However, Osborn and I concluded that the most plausible one was the "relative conventionality of the two metaphors."

> References to murder, strangling, death rattle, etc. are fairly common, especially among speakers and writers who oppose change in a political or economic system. Indeed, these expressions are trite to the extent that we would almost predict that a contemporary, conservative speaker would employ them when discussing the effects of a given proposal on existing political ideology. The sex metaphor, on the other hand, has not been so widely used that it has become predictable in an intense statement of attitude. It retains originality, which may, as Cicero says, appeal directly to the senses and stimulate mental processes. Thus, although the political science professor [using the sex metaphor] may have been no more intense in his statement of attitude toward the concept, he was more original than the economics professor [using the death metaphor]. This originality apparently enhanced audience assessment of his competence and trustworthiness. The economic professor's trite statement of attitude boomeranged. The metaphor detracted from audience assessment of his competence, trustworthiness, and ingenuity.[29]

In summary, our experiment's main contribution to rhetorical

heory was to provide rather convincing evidence that certain
inds of metaphors in certain kinds of situations do enhance
he persuasiveness of a speech. Their effects on judgments of
he speakers are complex, but apparently some types of meta-
hors detract from credibility, whereas others add to it.

Osborn won the argument. Does this victory constitute a
efeat for science? Of course it does not. It simply demonstrates
hat my inferences from a few scientific studies ignored the op-
ration of some relevant variables. In fact, Osborn's victory
vas, in a sense, also a victory for the scientific treatment of
ommunication. Without science, we probably could never
have settled the controversy to both our satisfactions.

   CRITICISM. The major criticism of the metaphor study was
hat the design gave us no way to compare directly the effects
f the two types of metaphor. Because the sex metaphor was
ased with the protective tariff concept only and the death
metaphor was used with the government aid to needy students
concept only, the differential effects of the two types could be
ttributed to other variables in the two basic speeches. A more
fficient design would have provided *both* a sex metaphor *and*
 death metaphor with which to conclude each speech. Al-
hough another dimension would thus be added to the design,
he rigor of the added directness of the evidence would have
made the extra complexity worthwhile.

FEAR APPEALS AND CREDIBILITY

In 1966 Gerald R. Miller and Murray A. Hewgill published
 series of studies examining the interaction of a speaker variable with a message variable on the attitudes of audiences.[30]
Methodologically and substantively, these studies are models
of communication scholarship, and the Speech Association of
America recognized their merit by awarding them a prize at
he 1967 convention in Los Angeles.

Some research had been done on the effectiveness of "fear"
or "threat" appeals in persuasive messages. Most of it had come
rom Irving Janis and his associates, who studied the results of

messages using "strong" and "weak" fear appeals in attempt to persuade people that they should take better care of their teeth.[31] In general, the difference between "strong" and "weak" appeals in these messages was that the weak appeals were abstract, the strong ones specific. A weak appeal would threaten tooth decay as the result of negligence about dental hygiene whereas a strong appeal would show unpleasant pictures of decaying teeth and gums. In their studies, Janis and his associates found that the mild appeals were more likely to result in the desired effect than were the strong ones. The researchers thought that the strong appeals were so unpleasant that the listeners tuned out, ignoring the recommendations along with the fear-arousing evidence. Thus, scholars in communication came to accept the generalization that mild fear appeals are more effective than strong ones.

Obviously, further work on fear appeals and their effects was important to communication research. Two considerations argued potently for more studies. Fear appeals cover an extremely wide range of persuasive behavior in contemporary American society. Reliable scientific conclusions about them would affect almost all social behavior, from child-rearing practices to national advertising systems. In addition, no specific kind of motivational appeal has been studied previously. Research on fear appeals thus is likely to be taken as a model for research on other kinds of motivational appeals.

Miller and Hewgill took significant steps toward filling this research gap. In their 1966 article, they reported three distinct approaches to fear appeals: (1) an examination of the interaction between fear appeals and source credibility with attitude change as the criterion; (2) a study of the relative effectiveness of making the referent of fear appeals "self" or "valued other" (wife and children); and (3) a preliminary investigation into susceptibility to specific fear appeals as a personality variable particularly relevant to communication research. Although all three approaches can be recommended, only the first will be considered here.

Miller and Hewgill started from a relatively strong theoretical base, as such bases go in communication research. At least our theorists have proposed "balance" or "congruity" or "consistency" formulations.[32] According to these theories, people are placed in a state of psychological discomfort when they are made aware that two or more of their cognitions (thoughts, feelings, beliefs) are incompatible. This discomfort, in general, leads to psychological action to remove or at least reduce the incompatibility.

This theory can be illustrated with a hypothetical example. Most of us have had, at one time or another, a favorite teacher or someone whom we have never detected committing an error—a person who has extremely high credibility for us. Suppose that we are also very devoutly religious. One day this teacher, responding to the questioning of a student, remarks: "I agree with those who say that religion is the opiate of the masses."

The remark throws us into a state of psychological discomfort, a state of imbalance, dissonance, and incongruity. The teacher's apparent religious beliefs are not compatible with our previous estimate of his credibility. Our discomfort is severe, for both the teacher's veracity and our religious beliefs are important to our behavioral systems.

What do we do about it? Clearly, at least five avenues of discomfort reduction are open to us:

1. We can deprecate the teacher's competence or trustworthiness, at least on this kind of topic, thereby keeping intact our religious beliefs.

2. We can change our religious beliefs to fit the teacher's, thereby preserving our faith in his veracity.

3. We can compromise between these two measures, slightly reducing our faith in both the teacher and religion and thus drawing the two closer together in our system of beliefs.

4. We can unconsciously distort the teacher's message, making it more compatible with our system of beliefs. For example, we might say: "He means nothing more than that church music has sort of a hypnotic effect."

5. We might react with incredulity, refusing to believe that

the message came from the teacher or accounting for i in such a way that it loses its seriousness. For example we might say: "The only reason he said that was to star an argument. That's one of his teaching techniques. H really doesn't believe it."

Which of these avenues to dissonance reduction we follow depends on a number of variables, some of which are extremely difficult to control.

Miller and Hewgill made what seems to be the reasonable assumption that strong fear appeals generate more psychological discomfort in audiences than do mild fear appeals. They accounted for the research that showed mild fear messages to be more effective in producing attitude change by bringing in another variable: source credibility.

Previous studies had left wide open an easy way to reduce psychological discomfort: deprecation of the source of the message. If a speaker is untrustworthy, we need not take what he says seriously. In their research, Miller and Hewgill controlled this way out for the listener by having as one of their experimental conditions a speaker with very high credibility a speaker whose competence and truthworthiness would be difficult to deprecate. Having closed this line of discomfort reduction, Miller and Hewgill hypothesized that listeners exposed to strong fear messages would respond by changing their attitudes more in the direction advocated than would listeners exposed to mild fear messages. The design included, then, two crucial manipulations: strength of fear appeal and source credibility.

The messages were persuasive speeches advocating certain civil defense measures, notably the building of underground schools. Miller and Hewgill defined their fear-arousal variable as follows:

While a mild fear-arousing message employs cues calculated to stimulate [incongruent] cognitions, . . . a strong fear message theoretically goes one step further and explicitly states the harmful consequences resulting from failing to change from conventional school buildings to underground schools. The message recipient is told that in case of natural disaster or nuclear attack his children will be slashed by flying glass, pinned under collapsed walls, or succumb to an agonizing death resulting from radiation sickness the symptoms of which are described in detail. [Audiences in the research were Parent-Teacher Association groups in Michigan.] Although these consequences are implicit in the mild fear message, they are not spelled out. This explicit detailing of harmful consequences is the basis for the assumption that the strong fear message will generate greater cognitive imbalance and, in turn, that this greater tension should strongly predispose the message recipient to behave *in some way* calculated to restore cognitive balance.[33]

Clearly, Miller and Hewgill's definition of the fear-arousal variable is compatible with previous definitions.

The procedures with regard to the other variable they manipulated in these studies, source credibility, were described as follows:

Variations in the taped introductions of the sources were used to manipulate initial credibility. The highly credible source was introduced as a professor of nuclear research recognized as a national authority on the biological effects of radioactivity. The low-credible source was introduced as a high school sophomore whose information was based on a social studies term paper and whose father was a contractor engaged in constructing underground schools. Credibility was measured by twelve, seven-interval, semantic-differential type scales chosen on the basis of prior factor analytic research by Berlo, Lemert, and Mertz. Six scales loading highly on competence and six loading highly on trustworthiness were used to assess those dimensions of credibility.[34]

Like the operational definition of fear appeals, the definition of source credibility was in line with other research on the same variable.

Miller and Hewgill tested in two studies the following three hypotheses, which, taken together, specify an interaction between strength of fear-arousing appeals and source credibility.

If a source has high credibility with a listener, appeals that elicit strong fear for persons highly valued by the listener will effect greater attitude change than appeals that elicit mild fear.

When presented by a low-credible source, a message containing strong fear-arousing appeals will result in lower recipient ratings of source credibility than a message containing mild appeals.

When the same messages are presented by a highly credible source, differences in recipient ratings of source credibility, if any, will favor the strong fear-arousing message.[35]

Miller and Hewgill's results clearly confirmed all three hypotheses. A strongly fear-arousing message from a highly credible source produced more attitude change than did a mild message. For less credible sources, a strongly fear-arousing message was no more effective than a mild message. Finally, postcommunication judgments of source credibility varied as Miller and Hewgill had predicted. A source initially high in credibility was rated higher after a strongly fear-arousing message than was the same source after a mild message. For the source initially low in credibility, the reverse was true. A strongly fear-arousing message from a source low in credibility resulted in even further deprecation of that source, whereas this effect was not nearly so pronounced for the same source when his fear appeals were mild.

SUMMARY

In this chapter, four actual series of studies in communication research have been discussed in some detail and brief allusion has been made to several others. The objectives of this discussion were to show that relatively sophisticated studies are within the competence of the beginner in the field and to illustrate, by describing actual research, the difficulties residing in rationales, definitions, methods of measurement, and interpretation. Criticisms of the studies were based on generalizations expressed earlier in this book.

Notes

1. For background, see Tamotsu Shibutani, *Improvised News: A Sociological Study of Rumor* (Indianapolis, Ind.: Bobbs-Merrill, 1966).

2. A good frame of reference is provided by H. Taylor Buckner, "A Theory of Rumor Transmission," *Public Opinion Quarterly*, XXIX (1965), 54–70.

3. Stuart C. Dodd, "Formulas for Spreading Opinions," *Public Opinion Quarterly*, XXII (1958–1959), 537–554.

4. For example, see Carl William Carmichael, "Attitude Change as a Function of the Relevance of Communications and Their Sources to Frustrating Experiences" (unpublished Ph.D. dissertation, University of Iowa, 1965), pp. 96–99.

5. The major study treated in this section is reported in two sources: Charles E. Osgood and Evelyn G. Walker, "Motivation and Language Behavior: A Content Analysis of Suicide Notes," *Journal of Abnormal and Social Psychology*, LIX (1959), 58–67; and Charles E. Osgood, "Some Effects of Motivation on Style of Encoding," in Thomas A. Sebeok (ed.), *Style in Language* (Cambridge, Mass.: M.I.T. Press, 1960), pp. 293–306.

6. Osgood, p. 297.

7. Osgood, p. 298.

8. Osgood, p. 298.

9. Osgood, p. 299.

10. Osgood, p. 299.

11. Osgood, p. 300.

12. Osgood, p. 300.

13. Osgood, p. 300.

14. Daniel M. Ogilvie, Philip J. Stone, and Edwin S. Shneidman, "Some Characteristics of Genuine Versus Simulated Suicide Notes," in Philip J. Stone, Dexter C. Dunphy, Marshall S. Smith, and Daniel M. Ogilvie, with associates, *The General Inquirer: A Computer Approach to Content Analysis* (Cambridge, Mass.: M.I.T. Press, 1966), pp. 527–535.

15. Ogilvie, Stone, and Shneidman, p. 534.

16. Osgood, p. 303.

17. Osgood, p. 305.

18. John Waite Bowers and Michael M. Osborn, "Attitudinal Effects of Selected Types of Concluding Metaphors in Persuasive Speeches," *Speech Monographs*, XXXIII (1966), 147–155.

19. Michael M. Osborn and Douglas Ehninger, "The Metaphor in Public Address," *Speech Monographs*, XXIX (1962), 223–234.

20. John Waite Bowers, "Language Intensity, Social Introversion, and Attitude Change," *Speech Monographs*, XXX (1963), 345–352.

21. John Waite Bowers, "Some Correlates of Language Intensity," *Quarterly Journal of Speech*, L (1964), 415–420; John Waite Bowers, "Influence of Delivery on Attitude Change toward Sources and Concepts," *Speech Monographs*, XXXII (1965), 154–158.

22. Bowers and Osborn, p. 147.

23. Bowers and Osborn, p. 148.

24. Bowers and Osborn, p. 148.

25. Bowers, "Some Correlates . . . ," p. 419.

26. Bowers, "Some Correlates . . . ," p. 420.

27. Bowers and Osborn, pp. 149–150.

28. Bowers and Osborn, p. 150.

29. Bowers and Osborn, p. 154.

30. Gerald R. Miller and Murray A. Hewgill, "Some Recent Research on Fear-Arousing Message Appeals," *Speech Monographs*, XXXIII (1966), 377–391.

31. Miller had summarized the research on fear appeals in an earlier article, "Studies on the Use of Fear Appeals: A Summary and Analysis," *Central States Speech Journal*, XIV (1963), 117–125. For an example of the type of research referred to, see Irving L. Janis and Seymour Feshbach, "Effects of Fear-Arousing Communications," *Journal of Abnormal and Social Psychology*, XLVIII (1953), 78–92.

32. Miller and Hewgill refer to Fritz Heider, "Attitudes and

Cognitive Organization," *Journal of Psychology*, XVL (1946), 107–114; Charles E. Osgood and Percy H. Tannenbaum, "The Principle of Congruity in the Prediction of Attitude Change," *Psychological Review*, LXII (1955), 42–55; Theodore Newcomb, "An Approach to the Study of Communicative Acts," *Psychological Review*, LX (1953), 393–404; and Leon Festinger, *A Theory of Cognitive Dissonance* (Stanford, Calif.: Row, Peterson, 1957).

33. Miller and Hewgill, p. 378.

34. Miller and Hewgill, p. 382.

35. Miller and Hewgill, pp. 380, 381.

4

A Note
on
Ethics
in
Communication
Research

This last chapter will discuss some aspects of a problem that confronts almost every communication scholar sometime during his productive career. The communication scientist's research has consequences, and he must face, *in advance,* as many of those consequences as he can foresee in order to decide whether his acts are ethical. If they are not, he should redesign his research or even find other projects.

The consequences of social research can be considered from two points of view: (1) Theoretically, research should bring us closer to scientific truth than we were previously. (2) For individual subjects, research may have a variety of kinds of short- and long-term effects, ranging from new knowledge (which may be true or false) to altered attitudes to very strong habits. This short chapter on ethics is not concerned particularly with the first kind of consequence. In fact, scientific validity is what the whole process is aimed at, and a scientist would not be a scientist if he did not pursue it. Man might make undesirable uses of the scientist's discoveries, and from an individual point of view a scientist might wish, in view of social consequences, that he had not pursued a certain kind of research. Nevertheless, he continues to pursue theory. He may try to influence man's use of the theory, but then he is acting as political, not scientific, man, and he has the same responsibilities as everybody else.

But the social scientist does have a problem as a scientist studying man when he chooses his research strategies and pursues his experimental designs. He has a responsibility to avoid long-term consequences that are unhealthy or nonadaptive to the individuals he studies. Otherwise, he may be destroying the very processes he is trying to illuminate. Furthermore, he may be building resistance to himself, his premises, and his method, as social scientists from the United States learned to their discomfort when they engendered the distrust of many Latin Americans in the late 1960s.[1]

Clarity requires an early note that the ethical question is not a particularly troublesome legal one to the social scientist. In order for him to be liable legally, at least if analogies from medical research hold true for him, the social scientist would have to be the instigator of some demonstrable damage to a subject resulting in financial loss or considerable misery. Such damage attributable to research manipulations is extremely difficult to prove. Even if an experimental subject can make a case connecting his misery to research procedures, the social scientist probably would not be liable if he could show that he took reasonable precautions to avoid such damage. Even then, he might be able to avoid liability if a group of experts in his field would testify that the knowledge to be gained from his research was worth the risk of damage. All of these generalizations, of course, are subject to legal reinterpretation. In fact, such reinterpretation seems likely, inasmuch as the questions have seldom been raised in the past.

In most communication research, experimental subjects undergo no treatments that are likely to lead to their damage or even discomfort. Most studies simply duplicate, with added controls, circumstances that are no more rigorous than those of everyday life. However, sometimes a communication scholar is interested in the effects of such variables as frustration, stress, deviation from norms, aggression, conformity pressures, and even demagoguery. Such variables make it especially necessary for him always to ask two questions: What consequences is my study likely to have for experimental subjects? How can I avoid any appreciable undesirable consequences? Two general topics will be discussed here: the use of children and other subjects especially susceptible to psychological change, and deceit and its implications.

HARMFUL EFFECTS

The communication scholar must exercise special care when he uses children or other susceptible subjects in his experiments. Children's habits are weak and can be modified relatively easily. Children cannot turn experimental manipulations on and off as mature subjects can.

Whenever a research problem demands the use of such subjects in a way that might be harmful, the scientist should consider two possible alternatives. First, he may be able to discover what he wants to discover by weakening an independent or dependent variable. In studies of frustration and aggression using children as subjects, for example, social scientists customarily make use of vicarious rather than direct and personal aggression. In other words, instead of being forced to witness actual violence, a child might be exposed to violent movie scenes. Instead of being put in a situation where he would be expected to hit another child, the subject might be placed in a room with humanlike toys, and his aggression toward the toys could be studied. Although the scientific statements warranted by such attenuated variables are not perfectly satisfactory, the risk of overgeneralization is not so great that it justifies scientific encouragement of personal aggression in children.

Second, the communication scholar might consider the possibility of attempting to generalize from field studies rather than from experiments. Irving Janis and his associates, for example, studied the antecedents and consequences of psychological stress by conducting extensive interview and questionnaire studies, using as their subjects surgical patients in hospitals.[2] The generalizations resulting from these studies enabled Janis to predict what kinds of patients would be most likely to suffer severe psychological discomfort as the result of surgery and to recommend some methods of presurgical communication that would alleviate this discomfort. Although field studies cannot be as scientifically sound as experiments, their use in studies where experimental manipulations probably would be harmful to individual subjects is made mandatory by ethical considerations.

DECEIT

A second ethical problem encountered by communication scholars is the frequent necessity to use deceit for experimental purposes. This problem is especially acute in studies of persuasion, where the persuasive message types to be tested are often composed of fictitious evidence and attributed to a nonexistent source. The principal danger, of course, is that these experimental messages will actually change the belief systems of subjects in undesirable directions.

The problem should be met in both of two ways. First, except when the persuasion attempt is a bona fide one (as in the studies of Gerald Miller and Murray Hewgill mentioned in Chapter 3), the experimenter should use as subjects only volunteers, not captive audiences. With appropriate planning, such volunteers are not difficult to obtain. In a college class, for example, if the teacher can be made sympathetic to the aims of communication research, almost every student will sign a well-designed volunteer form. The introduction of this form should be general enough that subjects later will not suspect that they are in experimental rather than real persuasive situations. Also, the form should specify the possibility that the experimental work may involve some psychological strain.

The Communication Research Laboratory in the Department of Speech and Dramatic Art at the University of Iowa uses a form like the following:

EXPERIMENTAL VOLUNTEER SIGN-UP SHEET

The Communication Research Laboratory conducts research to discover and test relationships among elements in communication situations. This research very often requires the cooperation of human subjects.

The Laboratory could not operate without the continued cooperation of college students willing to participate in experiments. These students add substantially to the knowledge available about communication processes.

We hope that you will indicate your willingness to cooperate by signing the attached sheet. [Where applicable, the Laboratory adds a sentence here about the rate of pay.]

Occasionally, communication experiments involve some psychological stress. To give you an idea of the kind of stress, we reproduce below a brief account of a study:

> In an experiment by Miller and Bugelski, subjects were told that they were working in an experiment on cooperation and competition, and by proper urging they were instigated to do their very best. Then they were paired, one at a time, with a partner who, they thought, was just another subject but who was actually a confederate of the experimenters. During "cooperation" this partner caused the subjects to fail by bungling his part of all the cooperative tasks. During "competition" the partner caused the subjects to fail by succeeding well himself and making distracting remarks and invidious comparisons. A variety of other little annoyances, such as mispronouncing the subject's name, were also provided.

Any experiment in which we ask you to participate probably will involve less stress than the one described above.

Please sign up below and on the next page with your name and telephone number.

This form is quite effective, especially if the person administering it stresses the value of communication research and promises minimum inconvenience in scheduling.

Any design in which deceit is employed should also have

as part of its normal procedure what some scholars have begun to call a debriefing session for all subjects. This session is simply an attempt to erase any cognitive effects the fictitious or distorted material may have had by explaining the aims of the research. It should be held as early after the criterion measures have been taken as is practical. Again, if this session is handled in an understanding way and if it stresses the value of the research and of the subjects' participation in it, almost everybody reacts with good nature.

SUMMARY

This short final chapter has discussed a few of the perennial ethical, human problems faced by experimental scholars in communication research. It did not supply all the answers to all the ethical questions, of course. Appropriate procedures to guard against damage to subjects must be devised for each study where stress or deceit is involved.

Notes

1. See various 1967 and 1968 issues of *Trans-action*, a periodical of the social sciences.

2. Irving L. Janis, *Psychological Stress: Psychoanalytic and Behavioral Studies of Surgical Patients* (New York: Wiley, 1958).

Selected Readings

Selected Readings

Barnlund, Dean C. (ed.). *Interpersonal Communication: Survey and Studies*. Boston: Houghton Mifflin, 1968. A good collection of communication studies, mostly experimental. Barnlund's summaries of experimental research in the introductions to the sections are excellent.

Bennis, Warren G., *et al.* (eds.). *Interpersonal Dynamics: Essays and Readings on Human Interaction*. Homewood, Ill.: Dorsey Press, 1964. Contains readings on leading topics of scientific concern ranging from the most rigorous experiments to a short story by John Cheever.

Berelson, Bernard. *Content Analysis in Communication Research*. New York: Free Press, 1952. A good introduction to the methods of content analysis, relatively nontechnical.

———, and Gary A. Steiner. *Human Behavior: An Inventory of Scientific Findings*. New York: Harcourt, Brace & World, 1964. Brief summaries of research in a wide variety of social sciences. Helpful as a reference but not very satisfying in itself.

Boring, Edwin G. *History, Psychology, and Science: Selected Papers*. New York: Wiley, 1963. Boring was a most literate philosopher and historian of science. His thought is rigorous, his style charming.

Braithwaite, Richard B. *Scientific Explanation: A Study of the Function of Theory, Probability and Law in Science*. Cambridge, England: Cambridge University Press, 1953. One of the standard sources on scientific method.

Brown, Roger. *Social Psychology*. New York: Free Press, 1965.

Brown analyzes some of the leading topics in social psychology, especially the psychology of language. He writes with a friendly style that is rare among social scientists.

Cronkhite, Gary L. *Persuasion*. Indianapolis, Ind.: Bobbs-Merrill, 1969. A full summary and ingenious analysis of research in persuasion.

Emmert, Philip, and William D. Brooks (eds.). *Communication Research Methodologies*. Boston: Houghton Mifflin, in press. A number of authors analyze the important methodological issues in communication research.

Feigl, Herbert, and May Brodbeck (eds.). *Readings in the Philosophy of Science*. New York: Appleton-Century-Crofts, 1953. A standard source on the philosophy of science.

Hovland, Carl I. (ed.). *The Order of Presentation in Persuasion*. New Haven, Conn.: Yale University Press, 1957. This item in the Yale series on attitude and communication was the first major work on organization written from a scientific point of view. It was the forerunner of more current research on inoculation to persuasion.

————, and Irving L. Janis (eds.). *Personality and Persuasibility*. New Haven, Conn.: Yale University Press, 1959. One of several in the Yale series of studies on attitude and communication. The series has been extremely important in giving respectability to the scientific study of communication.

————, Irving L. Janis, and Harold H. Kelley. *Communication and Persuasion: Psychological Studies of Opinion Change*. New Haven, Conn.: Yale University Press, 1953. A pioneering book in communication research, also available in a paperback edition (Yale, 1963).

Jakobovits, Leon A., and Murray S. Miron. *Readings in the Psychology of Language*. Englewood Cliffs, New Jersey: Prentice-Hall, 1967. An excellent collection of studies and theoretical statements on language behavior, with emphasis on problems of meaning.

Kerlinger, Fred N. *Foundations of Behavioral Research*. New York: Holt, Rinehart and Winston, 1967. An ambitious attack on problems in behaviorism, probably more quoted currently than any other foundations book.

Knapp, Peter H. (ed.). *Expression of the Emotions in Man*. New York: International Universities Press, 1963. Investigations of emotional behavior from the points of view embodied in a number of disciplines.

Krasner, Leonard, and Leonard P. Ullman (eds.). *Research in Behavior Modification*. New York: Holt, Rinehart and Winston, 1965. An excellent collection of studies on the application of operant conditioning theory to problems in behavior, especially communication behavior.

Miller, Gerald R. *Speech Communication: A Behavioral Approach*. Indianapolis, Indiana: Bobbs-Merrill, 1966. A behavioral analysis of some traditional problems in communication.

———, and Thomas R. Nilsen (eds.). *Perspectives on Argumentation*. Chicago: Scott, Foresman, 1966. Several of the chapters are behavioral analyses of traditional problems in argumentation.

Nilsen, Thomas R. (ed.). *Essays on Rhetorical Criticism*. New York: Random House, 1968. One chapter in the book, "The Pre-Scientific Function of Rhetorical Criticism," by John Waite Bowers, is relevant to science and communication.

Pool, Ithiel de Sola (ed.). *Trends in Content Analysis*. Urbana: University of Illinois Press, 1959. Reports of analytic studies, as well as an overview of the status of the method in the late 1950s.

Rosenberg, Milton J., and others. *Attitude Organization and Change: An Analysis of Consistency among Attitude Components*. New Haven, Conn.: Yale University Press, 1960. Another of the Yale studies on attitude and communication.

Saporta, Sol (ed.). *Psycholinguistics: A Book of Readings*. New York: Holt, Rinehart and Winston, 1961. Psycholinguistics is a hybrid offspring of psychology and linguistics. The studies in this book reflect the variety of research the discipline incorporates.

Sebeok, Thomas A. (ed.). *Style in Language*. Cambridge, Mass.: M.I.T. Press, 1960. A principally scientific collection of studies in stylistics.

Shibutani, Tamotsu. *Improvised News: A Sociological Study of Rumor*. Indianapolis, Indiana: Bobbs-Merrill, 1966. Rumor and its near relative, serial transmission of information, have been important topics for communication research since World War II. This book surveys the research conducted up to the mid-1960s.

Skinner, B. F. *Science and Human Behavior*. New York: Macmillan, 1953. Skinner is probably the most rigorously scientific analyst of behavior in the United States today. This book presents his general point of view.

———. *Verbal Behavior*. New York: Appleton-Century-Crofts, 1957. Skinner's analysis of verbal communication from the point of view of operant conditioning theory.

Skinner, B. F. *Walden Two*. New York: Macmillan, 1948. A novel that tells how society might be if it were organized and engineered by the Skinner brand of social scientist.

Smith, Alfred G. (ed.). *Communication and Culture: Readings in the Codes of Human Interaction*. New York: Holt, Rinehart and Winston, 1966. Probably the best anthology for students with a general interest in communication research.

Stone, Philip J., *et. al. The General Inquirer: A Computer Approach to Content Analysis*. Cambridge, Mass.: M.I.T. Press, 1966. Reports some excellent studies, though computer jargon is distracting.

Thibaut, John W., and Harold H. Kelley. *The Social Psychology of Groups*. New York: Wiley, 1959. A cost/reward system for the analysis of communication and other behavior in small groups.

Williams, Frederick. *Reasoning with Statistics: Simplified Examples in Communications Research*. New York: Holt, Rinehart and Winston, 1968. Williams avoids technicalities as much as he can. Still, the book is not easy reading.

Index

analysis of variance, 41–42

Becker, Samuel L., 112
Boring, Edwin G., 26, 27, 28

chance fluctuation in the dependent variable, 35; level of confidence or significance, 41–42; vocalization in prelanguage children as an example, 35–41
children as subjects in experiments, 130
Cloze procedure, 65; in study of suicide notes, 102

communication experiments: basic design, 32–35; effect of regional dialects in persuasive speeches, 61–63; effectiveness of fear-arousing messages and relation to source credibility, 119–124; more efficient designs, 47; metaphor efficacy, 111–119; rumor studies, 70–97; suicide note studies, 98–111; types of experiments, 63–64; vocalization in prelanguage children, 35–41; volunteer recruiting, 48–61
Conant, James, 27
content analysis, 63–64